A POSTMILLENNIAL PRIMER

BASICS OF OPTIMISTIC ESCHATOLOGY

P. ANDREW SANDLIN

ALSO BY P. ANDREW SANDLIN

Creational Worldview: An Introduction

Creational Marriage: Issues and Controversies

The Christian Sexual Worldview: God's Order in an Age of Sexual Chaos

Prayer Changes Things: Curing Timid Piety

The Full Gospel: A Biblical Vocabulary of Salvation

Religionless Christianity: Why the Faith in America is Toothless, Spineless, and Harmless

Crush the Evil: God's Promises Heal Man's Pessimism

Hindrances to Christian Culture

Evangelizing the Mind: Intellectual Good News for Culture and Church

Theological Presuppositions of Political Liberalism

Wrongly Dividing the Word: Overcoming the Law-Gospel Distinction

Make Christianity Great Again

ENDORSEMENTS

Can we not say that, more often than not, necessity is the driver of all application? As a pastor of a local church now in my third decade of vocational ministry, the pressing need to shepherd the flock of God by building up in the truth, exposing false ideas and ideologies, and warding off wolves often has driven me to find a biblical rationale to what I have often seen as practical obedience. To this end, I am newer to the postmillennial view, because in the ministry I have been pressed to find an eschatology which allows me to teach, train and live confidently before the Lord and the flock I am called to pastor. This, therefore, is the first book I have read specific to Postmillennialism and I am glad I did. As with other books by my friend Dr. P. Andrew Sandlin, this is written, not to the scholar, but to every Christian. It will be a great help for all of us seeking to apply God's word to all of life without the nagging guilt that somehow, we are not honoring God. In the midst of encroaching paganism, and the sad retreat of much of the evangelical (even Reformed) church from the threats of the state and woke culture, may you grow in your confidence in union with our Victorious Savior, the King Jesus Christ, who is moving history forward and onward to the final restoration of all things.

> ERIC ANDERSON, PASTOR, LIFESPRING CHURCH, CROSBY, MN

Sandlin does not offer utopian cliches befitting progressivism's eschatology of hysteria. Instead, he offers an articulate and sober biblical case for an eschatology of victory. It is readable and digestible for Christians, young and old.

> URIESOU BRITO, PASTOR, PROVIDENCE CHURCH, PENSACOLA, FL

From the first disciples of our Lord Jesus Christ until now, all Christians have joyously confessed, "[Christ Jesus] ascended to heaven and is seated at the right hand of God the Father almighty. From there, he will come to judge the living and the dead. . . . I believe in . . . the resurrection of the body, and the life everlasting." This indispensable twin belief in the bodily return of our Lord, who will raise the dead bodily, is, as Andrew Sandlin demonstrates, the affirmation that binds all Christians together despite their varied beliefs concerning *when* our Lord returns bodily. All Christians should welcome the expanded reprint of this concise book for at least two reasons. (1) The first 50 pages retain Sandlin's succinct presentations and critiques of the various "last days" belief systems among Evangelicals. In keeping with the book's title, he affirms an optimistic view of the "last days" with Christ's present reign expanding until "the last day" when Christ Jesus delivers the kingdom to the Father (1 Corinthians 15:22-25). (2) The additional pages beyond the initial 50 entail a fresh critical assessment of a contemporary heresy, the denial of the future bodily return of our present reigning Lord and of his raising the righteous bodily from their tombs.

> ARDEL B. CANEDAY, TEACHING ELDER,
> CHRIST BIBLE CHURCH, ST. PAUL, MN

When Jesus ascended on high, the Father said to him, "Sit at my right hand, until I make your enemies your footstool" (Ps. 110:1). Paul had this verse in mind when he said that Jesus will "deliver the kingdom to God the Father after destroying every rule and every authority and power. For he must reign until he has put all his enemies under his feet" (1 Cor. 15:23-24). We must understand that *this is the course of history,* Father and Son reigning in heaven, sending out Holy Spirit-empowered ambassadors into the rebellious provinces of their dominion who are tasked with proclaiming the Lordship of Christ and calling the rebels to the obedience of faith. To what extent will this mission be successful? In *A Postmillennial Primer,* Dr. P. Andrew Sandlin outlines the Scriptural reasons to expect far greater success than what many Christians have been led to believe. He calls us to look —and to *work* — for the day when "all the ends of the earth shall remember and turn to the Lord, and all the families of the nations shall worship before [him]" (Ps. 22:27)

> DOUG ENICK, PASTOR, TRINITY
> EVANGELICAL CHURCH, PRATT, KS

In this small monograph, Dr. P. Andrew Sandlin provides a tract for our times. He clearly shows Christians the way forward through the tangled thicket of fallen and failed humanistic culture. In just 70 pages he masterfully defines, declares, and defends the postmillennial hope as found in the Scriptures.

Sandlin opens by crisply and competently dismantling the opposing pessimistic eschatological systems. He exposes the central errors of dispensationalism, historic premillennialism, and amillennialism. Then having weighed these positions in the balance of Scripture and finding them wanting, he turns to his main concern: an introduction to the postmillennial hope. His method of approach is necessary in that postmillennialism is the most easily misunderstood and most widely assailed eschatological system in our modern context.

As R. J. Rushdoony notes in his original Preface, "The postmillennialist sees it as his duty to bring every area of life and thought into captivity to Christ, the Redeemer-King, so that He may rule over all things and bring in His reign of righteousness and peace through His people." As a noted culture warrior at the Center for Cultural Leadership, Sandlin is up to the task of presenting the postmillennial hope for the committed Christian in our troubled times.

If you want to know the basics of postmillennialism yourself or if you want to encourage others to consider it, this is the perfect treatise for both tasks. I highly commend this work to the concerned Christian. Good work, Dr. Sandlin!

KENNETH L. GENTRY, JR., TH.D.,
DIRECTOR OF GOODBIRTH MINISTRIES

To have the kind of eschatological optimism Andrew Sandlin describes in this potent work is simply another way we can affirm that we believe the Gospel, that we believe the Lord is sovereign, and that we believe He accomplishes all He sets out to accomplish. To have that kind of optimism means we will never again be able to pray, "Thy will be done on earth as it is in Heaven," without actually meaning it, believing it, and living it.

> GEORGE GRANT, PASTOR, PARISH
> PRESBYTERIAN CHURCH, FRANKLIN, TN

As a pastor I am consistently asked for good resources on postmillennialism to help someone understand this once prominent eschatological position. There are a number of thoroughly excellent books already available that I typically point people to, but they all require a good amount of time and investment to work through. I have not found a resource that is a quick, to-the-point, easily-read overview…until now! P. Andrew Sandlin's *Postmillennial Primer* is that book. It is just enough information to demonstrate why postmillennialism is the most biblical eschatological position, while also whetting your appetite to dig deeper and discover more. Reading this book will quickly reveal why eschatology matters.

> LUKE PIERSON, DISCIPLESHIP PASTOR,
> APOLOGIA CHURCH, MESA, AZ

This is an excellent introduction to postmillennialism. It gets to the heart of the issue and deals with the fundamental problems of dispensationalism. I particularly welcome Andrew's emphasis on the physical resurrection of the *body* on the Day of Judgement, which is what the Church has always confessed as the orthodox doctrine of the faith, but which has all too often been neglected and denied.

> STEPHEN C. PERKS, FOUNDER AND
> DIRECTOR, KUYPER FOUNDATION

Christian maturity requires us to surrender the puerile comfort of "panmillennialism" (it will all pan out in the end) and commence a thoughtful examination of eschatology. But where to begin? Dr. Sandlin's *Postmillennial Primer* provides clear, concise, Scripture-drenched insights into the future of Christ's victorious Church and glorious Kingdom. Waste no time on frustrating false starts in your end-time studies.

> DAVID SHAY, PASTOR, LIVING CHURCH,
> SUMMERVILLE, PA

Avoiding fanciful speculation as well as graphic-novel melodrama, Dr. Sandlin pens a sane, lucid, and most of all, faithfully edifying outline of the Bible's rich, hopeful, and optimistic eschatology. This is a welcome contribution for helping inoculate against the negative, reductionistic, and often depressing politicized and sexualized 24/7 hour news cycle — we live not in the CNN or the Fox News narrative, but in God's powerful, ruling, righteously redeeming narrative, a narrative that Christ's resurrection and ascension confirms and assures us that all things are becoming new. Eschatology is nothing less than how the entirety of the created order benefits from redemption accomplished and applied as far as the curse is found. Sandlin's careful and clear treatment expounds this truth with joy and conviction.

> JEFFERY J. VENTRELLA, JD, PHD,
> ARCHITECT OF THE BLACKSTONE LEGAL
> FELLOWSHIP

Copyright © 2023 by P. Andrew Sandlin

All rights reserved.

No part of this book may be reproduced in any form or by any electronic or mechanical means, including information storage and retrieval systems, without written permission from the author, except for the use of brief quotations in a book review.

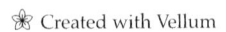

❦ Created with Vellum

To the memory of Greg L. Bahnsen
Postmillennial from pate to sole

EPIGRAPH

Power and Spirit now o'erflow,
  On me also be they pour'd,
  Till Thy last and mightiest foe
  Hath been made Thy footstool, Lord;
  Yea, let earth's remotest end
  To Thy righteous sceptre bend,
  Make Thy way before Thee plain,
  O'er all hearts and spirits reign!

GERHARD TERSTEEGEN (1697–1769)

CONTENTS

Preface — xix
David L. Bahnsen

Original Preface (1997) — xxi
Rousas John Rushdoony

Foreword — xxiii

Introduction — xxv

1. THE DEFECT OF DISPENSATIONALISM — 1
   The Bible Interprets Itself — 2
   The Bottom Line of Dispensationalism — 4
   Conclusion — 19

2. THE PROBLEM OF PREMILLENNIALISM — 21
   A Summary of the Premillennial View — 22
   The Premillennial Problem — 23
   Conclusion — 24

3. THE ANOMALY OF AMILLENNIALISM — 25
   The Old Testament Predicts a Godly Golden Age on Earth — 26
   The New Testament Verifies, Not Reverses, The Kingdom Promises — 29
   Kingdom Promises That Must Pertain to the Entire Earth — 31
   Conclusion — 32

4. THE PROMISE OF POSTMILLENNIALISM — 33
   Passages That Promise a Great, Extended Era of Earthly Peace, Prosperity and Holiness — 34
   Passages That Promise the Incremental Advancement of God's and Ghrist's Kingdom in Human History — 35
   Passages That Promise the Unique and Potent Presence of God Accompanying and Energizing His Covenant People in Their Kingdom-Advancing Commission — 46
   Conclusion — 48

5. CONFESSIONAL POSTMILLENIALISM — 49
   Confessions Not Millennially Agnostic — 50
   The Postmill Brits — 52
   Conclusion — 53

6. CREEDAL ESCHATOLOGY IS BIBLICAL ESCHATOLOGY — 54
   Heretical Preterism — 55
   Orthodox Biblical Eschatology — 57
   Conclusion — 65

Epilogue: Why We Will Win — 67
Notes — 73
Bibliography — 79
About the Center for Cultural Leadership — 81
About the Author — 83

PREFACE

DAVID L. BAHNSEN

When I found out that Andrew Sandlin was re-publishing *A Postmillennial Primer* I became excited, not merely to read it once again (I am quite sure I have read it a half-dozen times), but excited to have a new and updated deliverable product that I could pass out conveniently to those curious about the postmillennial perspective. There exists plenty of great literature defending this vital and biblical eschatological outlook, but the challenge has always been getting people to understand *why* they need to read about the topic at all! This primer does exactly that.

The cause of an optimistic eschatology has never been one of enlightening one's view of the future as much as informing their activity in the present. The problem with the topic of end times is that it is messy, it is nuanced, it requires various hermeneutical commitments that are not always a given, and most of all, it depends upon one having a Biblical curiosity in such things. Casual conversations are a hard way to drive interest in this topic because people understandably want the conclusion laid out without having diligently walked through the premises. A long-form book is a tough way to incentivize eschatological precision because there is inadequate motivation to work through the subject if one is not sure why their understanding needs enhancement. This primer, though, is a powerful way to introduce the topic, guide the reader through a basic overview that is compelling and motivational, yet not exhaustive or complete.

Andrew does the work of a theologian in utilizing key biblical texts to at least provoke further thought. He offers a gentle but compelling critique of other eschatological systems that too many accept without adequate examination. He connects the dots in the hermeneutical framework that may lead one to a postmillennial eschatology. And he does this on a foundation of covenant theology. It is faithful, compelling, and most of all, inspiring.

What is it, you ask, that could be inspiring about this work and this topic? Well, in a day and age of unending temptation towards retreat, mediocrity, surrender, and escape, all of which may feel warranted at times, this primer makes the case for an eschatology that abandons the Benedict Option, and instead pursues the Psalm 110 Option. It inspires believers to appreciate what we have inherited, why it matters, and to examine the reason for perseverance in times of cultural exasperation. It roots our basis for optimism and hope in Scripture, and drives us towards a cohesive theology that sees victory in the resurrection, not in the end of the world.

Postmillennialism is not an academic exercise; it is a practical framework for living out our heavenly prayer, "Thy Kingdom Come, they will be done, on earth, as it is in Heaven."

ORIGINAL PREFACE (1997)

ROUSAS JOHN RUSHDOONY

While *eschatology* means the doctrine of *last* things, it can with justice be said that it necessarily means also *first* things. No man gets on a plane, train, or bus and decides on his destination after boarding it. He must first of all have a destination.

The same is true in the life of faith. To begin without a destination, an eschatology, is nonsense. Well over half a century ago, I knew slightly an able pastor who called himself a panmillennialist, i.e., he believed in all views and in none. He was a particularly able and powerful speaker but also an impotent one. He selected sermon texts in terms of current interests, appealing subjects, and concerns over increasing his stature. He was always interesting to hear but always without a focus. He did well but he was in essence a dry well because he was maintaining a church, not creating an army for the Lord. His lack of an eschatology was a lack of purpose.

The premillennial preacher wants to save souls before the "rapture" comes. The amillennialist preacher seeks to save souls as brands from the burning, as men rescued into the church, God's ark, from the floods of evil. The postmillennialist sees it as his duty to bring every area of life and thought into captivity to Christ, the Redeemer-King, so that He may rule over all things and bring in His reign of righteousness and peace through His people.

Our Lord's commandment, "seek ye first the kingdom of God, and his righteousness" or justice (Mt. 6:33), is an eschatological statement. The Bible from start to finish has an end in view and is governed by God's plan and purpose. To attempt to promote a biblical faith without the biblical purpose is false and untenable. The biblical God does not muddle through, improvising as he goes, and for Christians to assume that eschatology is unimportant is to say that it is unimportant what we believe about first and last things.

With some, a lack of eschatological concern is simply selfishness, egocentricity. Their attitude is, I am saved, so I am going to heaven; therefore to be concerned about end times is not necessary for me. Such a view is a tacit denial of Christianity; we are not called simply to avoid hell and to float to heaven "on flowery beds of ease," but to serve God with all our heart, mind, and being, and our neighbor as ourselves. The focus of our salvation is not to escape hell but to serve our Lord and seek *first* his Kingdom.

The eschatology of death governs the non-Christian world. Men see death as the end of life, and the grave as its effective goal. They live in order to get out of life what they can while they can. The non-millennialist is in his own way a part of this egocentric world.

I therefore strongly commend Andrew Sandlin's brief but telling study. Our faith must be eschatological or it will be impotent. An impotent Christian faith is a contradiction in terms.

FOREWORD

This primer is a slightly revised reprint of the same 1997 title published by the Chalcedon Foundation. Chapters 5 and 6 are new, though elsewhere published. This booklet is neither definitive nor exhaustive. It doesn't marshal every argument for or refute every objection to postmillennialism. In the bibliography you can find works to explore the topic in greater detail.

I'm sometimes asked the best place in the Bible to start for proving postmillennialism. I reply, "Genesis 1:1." An optimistic eschatology rests in an optimistic protology. The sovereign Creator fashioned a very good creation that will fulfill his kingdom-expanding dominion purposes in time and history. (See my book *Creational Worldview: An Introduction*.)

This primer shows what an optimistic eschatology looks like.

INTRODUCTION

This primer is about eschatology.[1] Eschatology, as I am using the term, means the study of God's plan for the future. This monograph will deal with other issues only as they touch on eschatology. In chapter 1, for instance, I will address matters like the Abrahamic Covenant and David's throne, but I do not intend to give these and related issues a thorough treatment. I mention them only to demonstrate my thesis: that dispensationalism is false, and postmillennialism is true.

This primer is written for interested pastors, lay Christians, and students; though it is substantial enough for the scholar, it does not require specialized training in theology or languages. The postmillennial position outlined in this primer does not rest on a particular textual reading or the correct treatment of any of these other issues. This book may be read and studied profitably by pastors, seminarians, collegians, other students (even high school students), intelligent laymen, and interested housewives. Because the nature of this booklet is biblical and, to a lesser extent, theological, I will not address the historical issues: for example, how the various millennial viewpoints arose and have developed in the church, which sectors of the church have affirmed which viewpoints, or how the viewpoints have affected each other. For issues related to these and other topics, I recommend D. H. Kromminga's *The Millennium in the Church*.

This monograph will not deal extensively with amillennial or historic (nondispensational) premillennialism. I will spend considerably more time refuting dispensationalism than either historic premillennialism or amillennialism. There are two reasons for this: first, dispensationalism has been the leading eschatological view among Protestant conservatives in the modern world, and second, it is more defective in its understanding of the Bible and more injurious in its implications than either historic premillennialism or amillennialism.

We should never develop an eschatological agnosticism, or, as some humorously call it, panmillennialism: "It'll all pan out in the end." Different eschatological views lead to different practices. For example, if we believe that the world is predestined to doom and destruction (at least until the Second Advent), we will be less likely to work for the evangelization and Christianization of the world. If we assume that the world must be Christianized before Christ returns, we will be less eager for an any moment "rapture" of the church. If we hold that the Old Testament (OT) Jewish promises are not fulfilled in the New Testament (NT) church, we will be disinclined to maintain the enthusiasm and optimism recipients of those glorious promises would naturally maintain.

Eschatology is not a test of Christian fellowship, since it is not at the heart of the gospel. It is, however, a vital aspect of a full-orbed Faith; and whoever is wrong about eschatology is likely to be wrong in other areas of thought and life.

CHAPTER 1
THE DEFECT OF DISPENSATIONALISM

I DON'T INTEND to offer in this chapter a comprehensive disproof of dispensationalism; after all, this is a primer, not a textbook. To those who desire such extensive disproof, I recommend Oswald Allis's *Prophecy and the Church*, which, although now almost 80 years old, might be the most devastating refutation of classic dispensationalism ever produced in a single volume. In fact, unless one is already committed to dispensationalism, it's hard to imagine anyone's reading that book without being persuaded by Allis's utterly impregnable disproof of dispensationalism.

Two more recent books I'll mention are John Gerstner's *Wrongly Dividing the Word of Truth: A Critique of Dispensationalism* and Vern Poythress' *Understanding Dispensationalists* (see the bibliography).

My aim, rather, is to exhibit how the very foundational teaching of classic dispensationalism, not the peripheral issues, cannot be true. If it can be shown that the structural foundation is unsound, the edifice of dispensationalism can't stand (Mt. 7:26, 27). It also shouldn't go without mentioning in a primer on postmillennialism that the 19th century theological founder of dispensationalism, J. N. Darby,[1] developed his system partly in reaction against the postmillennialism of his teachers at Trinity College, Dublin.[2] Dispensationalism is rooted partly in *anti*-postmillennialism.

Over the last few decades, some dispensationalists have gradually shed various distinctives of their classic system. They have given this revision names like "progressive dispensationalism."[3] In some cases the revision has been so pronounced that it's hard to distinguish it from basic covenant theology (the theological system assumed in this primer[4]).

I address here classic dispensationalism since its distinctives retain their popularity, largely outside most traditionally dispensational seminaries, which no longer find the classical formulation of that system biblically tenable. But plenty of Christians still hold to a "pop" dispensationalism and its distinctives like the inevitable apostasy of the present age, an imminent rapture of the church, and a subsequent seven-year tribulation period gradually governed by the antichrist and beast of Revelation. This eschatology might even still be the majority report among professing evangelicals. For that reason alone it's worth considering.

THE BIBLE INTERPRETS ITSELF

A supreme interpretive irony of dispensationalism is that, while it denies in the most vehement terms the eternal authority of the Old Testament law[5] it affirms with equal vehemence the most literal interpretation of Old Testament prophecy.[6] There is a powerful reason for this: *Dispensationalism is primarily an eschatological system, not an ethical system.* It is a philosophy of history, not a program of behavior. The danger of the irony is that while the NT does confirm, in large measure, the authority of OT law,[7] it does not, in large measure, interpret OT prophecy literally. Dispensationalists have things just backwards. They deny the authority of OT law while affirming the literalness of OT prophecy.

From the very beginning, the Christian church grasped this point about OT prophecy. As Pelikan observes, "There was no early Christian who simultaneously acknowledged the doctrinal authority of the Old Testament and interpreted it literally."[8] He did not interpret it literally because Christ himself and his apostles did not interpret it literally. This has been the approach of orthodox Christianity historically. Allis, in his masterly critique of dispensationalism, stated:

> The doctrine of the Christian Church, as generally accepted, has always been that the New Testament takes precedence over the Old, that Christ and His apostles are the authoritative interpreters of the Old Testament, that its shadows and types are to be interpreted in the light of the clearer gospel revelation.[9]

In the same vein, Gerstner observes that a literal interpretation of Israel in the OT era undercuts the unity of the Bible:

> We have already noted that, historically speaking, this dispensational denial of the unity of Israel and the church represents a surprising novelty. From the earliest period of Christian theology onward, the essential continuity of Israel and the church has been maintained. This historic doctrine of the church is based on both the clear implication of Old Testament texts and the clear teaching of the New Testament.[10]

Orthodox Christianity sees in the OT not a separate theological or prophetic revelation to be examined in isolation, but as the authoritative prelude to the completion of revelation in the NT. For this reason, the only place to locate the key for interpreting prophecy (and other forms of biblical revelation) *is the Bible itself*. This would seem to be self-evident. It is not, however, the dispensational scheme. For dispensationalists it is not the NT, but *literalness*, that is the basis of biblical interpretation. This is an example of imposing an external, alien scheme on the Bible. Instead, we should allow the Bible to show us how it interprets itself. When we do that, we discover that the dispensational system of theology is untenable. That is why their literal-only interpretive key is essential to dispensationalists: their interpretive scheme is necessary to support their theological conclusions.

THE BOTTOM LINE OF DISPENSATIONALISM

It is imperative to recognize that the pretribulational (or midtribulational or posttribulational or partial or secret) "rapture," the "seven (or ten or fifteen) dispensations," the "seven-year tribulation period," the "parenthesis church," the "Mark of the Beast," the "regathering of Israel," and other dispensational distinctives are not central to its system. Charles Ryrie, a leading defender of dispensationalism, states: "The essence of dispensationalism, then, is the distinction between Israel and the church."[11] All of these other distinctives flow from the one central distinctive — the denial that the multiracial church of the NT replaces OT ethnic Israel as the single people of God and is the heir of its covenant promises (and curses). Ryrie notes further:

> A dispensationalist keeps Israel and the Church distinct.... This is probably the most basic theological test of whether or not a man is a dispensationalist, and it is undoubtedly the most practical and conclusive. A man who fails to distinguish Israel and the Church will inevitably not hold to dispensational distinctives; and one who does, will.[12]

It's important to mention that by "distinction" Ryrie and other dispensationalists don't mean mere physical distinctions. Nondispensationalists agree with dispensationalists that racial Jews are always physical Jews, and racial Gentiles are always physical Gentiles; God in salvation doesn't change people's race any more than he changes their sex or color.

Rather, dispensationalists argue that the chief distinction between Israel and the church *is in God's plan and program.* The NT church is seen as a separate entity from the OT church (Ac. 7:38), having separate promises and a separate calling.[13] The racial "distinction," according to dispensationalists, means that the new covenant church has not replaced old covenant Israel as the true people of God, while nondispensationalists hold that this distinction does not lead to dispensational conclusions.

Dispensationalism denies that the church is the True Israel. The key tenet of dispensationalism, as Ryrie observes, is the distinction between ethnic Israel and the multiracial NT church; this is the defect of dispensationalism. Therefore, *to refute this premise is to refute dispensationalism.*

I will set forth *five* clear, biblical evidences that the new covenant church has replaced old covenant Israel as the covenant people of God, and in so doing refute "the essence of dispensationalism" (Ryrie). Three of the five evidences involve a NT interpretation of OT teaching.

There is only one olive tree of God's redemptive blessing, indicating one people of God (Rom. 11:13-24)[14]

Paul's burden in Romans 11 is to prove that God has not definitively concluded his dealings with ethnic Israel (v. 1). Since God has taken his kingdom from the Jews and given it to all Christians, both ethnic Jew and Gentile (Mt. 21:43-45), Christians may have gotten the impression that he no longer cares for ethnic Jews and has no plan whatever for them. Paul uses the symbolism of the olive tree to correct that idea. The Jews as a nation are compared to the natural branches of a divinely cultivated olive tree (v. 21). The olive tree denotes God's blessings of eternal salvation (v. 26) and his covenant dealings (v. 27). Ethnic Israel was originally God's specially loved, sovereignly selected covenant people. Because of their unbelief, however, these Jewish branches were severed from the olive tree (v. 20).

Gentile Christians in the new covenant era are compared to "wild [uncultivated] branches" engrafted to replace the discarded natural branches of Israel (v. 19). Paul makes clear that this dual action of discarding the unbelieving natural branches of Israel and replacing them with the believing wild branches of Gentile believers is based solely on the sovereign grace of God (vv. 30-36).

Paul's main point of this analogy, however, is to assure his readers that God hasn't permanently discarded the Jews; they will one day be restored to the place of blessing they once held. (This does not promise that Israel as a nation or political body will be restored; rather, it denotes that a multitude of Jews will be converted and brought into the church.)

The promise of vv. 11, 12, 23-25 is that one day the calling of the Gentiles in the present era will provoke the Jews to jealousy, and they will then believe in great number. The Jews are not permanently eliminated in God's covenantal and redemptive plan; an overwhelming number will be saved. In turn, this wholesale salvation of the Jews will produce many *additional* conversions among the Gentiles;[15] there will be a "snowball" effect of conversions. This teaching, by the way, conforms to the postmillennial expectation (see chapter 4).

The main point to recognize for our purpose in this chapter, however, is that there is *one* olive tree. The fatness and grace and benefit that the Gentiles derive is the *same* fatness and grace and benefit the ethnic Jews were designed to derive, but forfeited by their unbelief and disobedience. The wild branches of the new covenant, multinational and multiracial church have *replaced* the natural branches of ethnic, national Israel as the single people of God.

Some dispensationalists refer to this fact negatively as "replacement theology."[16] What they should grasp is that "replacement theology" is orthodox *Christian* theology: believers replace unbelievers in God's covenant plan. God has a single way of redemptive and covenant blessing. It is not the Jewish way or the Gentile way, but the *Christian* way.

Had God intended to assert that the new covenant church has *not* replaced old covenant Israel, as dispensationalists teach, but that the two remain separate and distinct peoples whom he deals with differently, it is hard to imagine a more *inappropriate, senseless* analogy he could have used to express this fact. A single olive tree of divine election and covenant blessing denotes a single people of God. This is just what the analogy teaches: not two olives trees but *one* olive tree with natural, cultivated, Jewish branches that have been discarded and will one day be restored, and wild, uncultivated, Gentile branches that have been grafted in.

This passage does not teach that there is a distinction between Israel and the church. Rather, it teaches that the church has become in God's plan *what Israel once was:* God's sovereignly elected, specially loved people who are the recipients of his covenantal dealings. The new covenant church, having replaced ethnic Israel, is the covenant people of God.

2. Jew and Gentile are both Abraham's seed if they are united to Christ (Gal. 3:29), and therefore entitled to the blessings of the Abrahamic covenant (Gal. 3:16 [Gen. 13:14-16, 15:5, 17:7, 8]; Eph. 2:11-13, 19, 20) [17]

The Abrahamic covenant is a leading feature of the OT.

Both dispensationalists and nondispensationalists agree on this.[18] It involves glorious promises to Abraham about him and his seed. He was a pagan in a pagan nation when God sovereignly selected him as the recipient of divine love and grace (Gen. 11:27-12:5). What are the chief provisions of the Abrahamic covenant? They are four: a relationship, a land, a seed (posterity), and a blessing (to the other nations). Three are expressed plainly in Gen. 17:7, 8:

> *And I will establish my covenant between me and thee and thy seed after thee in their generations for an everlasting covenant, to be a God unto thee and to thy seed after thee. And I will give unto thee, and to thy seed after thee, the land wherein thou art a stranger, all the land of Canaan, for an everlasting possession; and I will be their God.*

We can observe in this passage the first three provisions: relationship (God would be a God to Abraham), land (Canaan), seed (to whom God would also be a God and give the land as a possession).

The fourth provision, that Abraham and his seed would bless the nations of the earth (or that in Abraham they would bless themselves), is found in the first mention of the Abrahamic covenant (Gen. 12:2, 3).

Throughout the OT, this covenant and its provisions keep coming up (*e.g.,* Lev. 26:42-45; Dt. 1:8, 4:31; Ps. 105:8·10; Is. 29:22, 23; Jer. 34:17-20; Ezek. 33:24; Mic. 7:18-20). God would be a God to Israel (the new name given to Jacob, Abraham's grandson) and Israel as a nation would be his people; God would give (or return to) them a land (Canaan); he would be the God to their seed and give their seed the land; finally, that seed would bless the other (Gentile) nations of earth.

This covenant had a "token," or sign: circumcision (Gen. 17:11; called a "sign" and a "seal" in the NT [Rom. 4:11]). It was so vital that the token was equated with the covenant itself (Gen. 17:10; note also Ac. 7:8): any Israelite who was not circumcised was to be executed (Gen. 17:14). Circumcision marked out the seed of Abraham to whom the covenant promises would apply (vv. 12, 13).

But is the seed of Abraham only the physical seed of the Jews? What about the Gentiles who became religious Jews? Were they entitled to the promises of the Abrahamic covenant? Of course, they were (Gen. 17: 12, 13; Ex. 12:43-49). The covenant promises are based on covenant inclusion, and *God decides who is included in the covenant.* For this reason he could exclude Ishmael (Gen. 17:17-21), though he was the physical seed of Abraham, while God *included* any Gentile males who became circumcised, though they were not of the physical seed of Abraham. Male Gentiles became the seed of Abraham by undergoing the rite of circumcision and thereby became Jews.

Dispensationalists tend to stress the Abrahamic covenant made with him and his seed as limited to the physical seed of ethnic Israel. But as we have seen, even the OT refutes that notion. Gentiles were welcome to join the nation, appeal for circumcision, and therefore become covenant members (Ex. 12:43-49). The covenant is governed *fundamentally* by religion, not race.

This was true in the OT, although it has become more prominent in the NT era (Eph. 2:11-22). In fact, a primary difference between the old covenant and the new covenant is that Gentiles no longer need be circumcised and become Jews in order to become the covenant people of God (Ac. 15:1f; Gal. 5:2, 3). There is a reason for this: *all who are united to Christ by faith are now the seed of Abraham.*

Galatians 3 makes abundantly clear that the seed of Abraham toward which the OT pointed is Jesus Christ (v. 16). Just as Christ is identified as the true heir of David's throne in the Davidic covenant (Ac. 2:25-36), so he is identified as the true seed of the Abrahamic covenant.

The point of Galatians 3 is that the Abrahamic covenant is not primarily racial, but religious (again, this was true even in the OT, though less prominent). The Abrahamic covenant pertains not to the Jewish rites and ceremonies or even the Mosaic law (Gal. 3:17),[19] but to the sovereign election by God of his people, all of whom are united by faith to Christ (v. 16, 29).

Just as David's physical seed to whom the throne of Israel was promised (2 Sam. 7) prefigured and pointed to the true royal seed, Christ (Ac. 2:29-36), so Abraham's physical seed to whom the glorious covenant pledges of relationship, land, seed, and blessing were given prefigured and pointed to the true Abrahamic seed, Christ.

Because, however, dispensationalists don't allow the NT to interpret the OT, they maintain a distinction between Israel and the church which the NT will not permit. This is despite the fact Jesus himself did not identify the seed of Abraham with mere physical lineage, but with those who exercise the faith and practice of Abraham (Jn. 8:39, 40).

Of course, dispensationalists may wish to counter that while it is true that the NT proves that the Abrahamic covenant includes saved Gentiles as the recipients of that covenant, it is not true that the Abrahamic covenant is equivalent to the church. The problem with this (dealt with below) is that Paul elsewhere specifically identifies the church with the "commonwealth of Israel" and "the covenants of promise" (Eph. 2:12; cf. 1:23, 2:19-22), and therefore sees the new covenant church as the recipient of the promises of the Abrahamic covenant.

But if this is the case, then the dispensationalist notion of a fundamental distinction between Israel and the church cannot be true. Ethnic Israel traces its racial and religious lineage to Abraham; but, according to Christ and Paul, Abraham is father *only* to those who by faith belong to Christ, whether ethnic Jew *or* Gentile. *Christians are the true seed of Abraham.*

The Abrahamic covenant cuts across all racial barriers. It did even in the OT, but does increasingly in the NT. This means that we cannot maintain a distinction between Israel as one people of God, and the church as another people of God, as dispensationalism likes to do. And since this supposed distinction, according to Ryrie the "essence of dispensationalism," is refuted by the teaching of Jesus and Paul, dispensationalism cannot be true.

If the seed of Abraham includes Christ and all united to him by faith as Galatians teaches; if this seed of Abraham is entitled to the promises of the Abrahamic covenant (relationship, land, seed, blessing — see below); and if the provisions of the Abrahamic covenant which were once limited to those who were (or became by circumcision) ethnic Jews now embraces all united to Christ by faith, it follows that the dispensationalist distinction between Israel and the church — the "essence of dispensationalism," in Ryrie's words — cannot be valid.

And if it is not valid; neither is dispensationalism.

To expand on one of the more contentious points above: if regenerate Gentiles are heirs of the Abrahamic covenant, they are entitled to its promises. It's not possible to argue as some dispensationalists do that Christians are entitled to some but not all of the promises, or that there are two seeds of Abraham, the very idea Paul explicitly denies (Gal. 3:16).

I once pointed out this fact to a dogged dispensationalist. His response was, "The Gentiles get the spiritual promises, but not the physical promises, which belong to the Jews." Such dualistic thinking cannot be supported by the Bible. He should have known that it is impossible to separate the physical promises from the spiritual promises (in the Bible, "spiritual" does not mean non-physical), and nothing in the NT modifies this fact, except that the land promises are expanded (see chapter 4). The covenantal promises to which Galatians 3:16, 29 teaches the church is entitled cannot exclude a certain portion of those promises without good warrant. *Believing Gentiles are entitled to all to which believing Jews are entitled.*

This is clear not only from Galatians 3:29, but also Ephesians 2:11-13, 19, 20. In this passage Paul assures his Gentile readers that while before their conversion they were set outside Israel's commonwealth and therefore God's covenantal plan (Eph. 2:12), now that they are converted, they are heirs of the Jews' salvation, covenants and promises (2:13-19). God has united converted Jews and Gentiles into his covenant plan, tearing down the racial hostility between them (v. 15).

Before Christ's redemptive work on the cross, Gentiles were required to become Jews in order to gain the benefits of the Abrahamic covenant. Now they gain access to the Abrahamic covenant solely by faith in Christ. There is no need for them to join racial, national Israel in order to become the seed of Abraham and obtain the promises of the Abrahamic covenant.

But obviously, if the converted Jews *and* Gentiles of the new covenant church are the heirs to the promises of the Abrahamic covenant, then the new covenant church has replaced old covenant Israel as God's chosen people. And if the new covenant church has become God's new chosen covenant people, there can be no distinction between Israel and the church such as dispensationalists suppose.

3. *The NT teaches that the new covenant is fulfilled in the present age (Jer. 31:27-34; Ezek. 37:15-28; Lk. 22:20; Heb. 8:7-13; 10:12-18; 2 Cor. 3:6)*[20]

The OT prophesies of a time when God will insert this law into the hearts of "the house of Israel," forgive and put away their sins definitively, and regenerate an overwhelming number (this is another support for postmillennialism). The passages in Jeremiah and Ezekiel are only two of the most prominent. This is identified as the "new covenant." In every case mentioned in the OT, this refers explicitly to Israel or the Jews as its recipients; it does not once state or imply that the Gentiles or a church including Gentiles *as Gentiles* will enjoy the new covenant. The new covenant is important for our purposes because it is mentioned prominently several times in the NT.

If we were reading only the OT, we would be obliged to agree with the dispensationalist that the new covenant is made only of ethnic Israel, the physical seed of Abraham (and Gentiles who joined national Israel).

But we must read all of the Bible to discover God's teaching on any topic. And it is important to read the OT in light of the NT, a later (though certainly not more accurate or superior) revelation. The NT is no more authoritative than the OT, and it does not give a higher ethical or instructional standard than the OT; but the NT does give a more complete picture of God's will than the OT. This is the case with the new covenant. It is a prime example of how we need to let the NT interpret the OT.

The first intimation that "Israel" or "the house of Jacob" mentioned in the OT as the exclusive recipients of the new covenant may not mean only national, ethnic Jews is found in our Lord's' institution of communion at the last Supper (Lk. 22:20). On that intimate occasion with his disciples, he identifies his future shed blood on the cross (as symbolized by the fruit of the vine) with the new covenant. Our present purpose is not to explore the significance of this identification. Rather, it is to note how this identification defines (or redefines) the OT recipients of the new covenant. For we can hardly surmise that when Christ implied that his blood-shedding death inaugurated the new covenant, he meant to limit that covenant to physical, national Jews. In several parables, he had already taught that God intended to suspend his dealings with an unbelieving and rebellious Israel and turn to believing Gentiles (Mt. 20: 1-16; 21:28-45; 22:1-14, 23:34-39). Christ had made abundantly clear that the benefits of his redemptive work were not to be limited to national, ethnic Jews, and the Pharisees understood and deeply resented this teaching (Mt. 21:45, 46).

More obvious proof that the beneficiaries of the new covenant included all the people of God, believing Jew and Gentile, is the fact that the new covenant meal was routinely celebrated by all Christian churches (1 Cor. 11:20-34). The new covenant blood-bond which the communion wine signifies is made with all who come to the table in faith, that is, Christ's church.

Similarly, Paul in 2 Corinthains 3:6 designates himself as the minister of the new covenant. What is perhaps most significant about this passage is how Paul contrasts his own ministry of the new covenant with Moses' ministry of the old covenant (v. 13, 14). The new covenant ministry to the church is much more glorious than the old covenant ministry to Israel alone (this theme is greatly expanded in the Epistle to the Hebrews).

Paul points out that the eyes of most Jews are blinded to the meaning of the OT (vv. 14, 15), and that when the Jews turn to Christ, that blinding will be removed (v. 16). This is most crucial for our study. Paul seems to be saying that the new covenant was intended *all along* to refer to God's redemptive pledge in Christ in which all the church, not just converted Jews, would participate, but that because the Jews do not trust Christ, they do not understand the OT meaning. The ceremonial laws in particular had a "built-in obsolescence," an "expiration date."[21] Paul, minister to the multinational church, is the minister of the new covenant, the meaning of which unbelieving Jews do not grasp.

Finally, we note the reiteration of the new covenant twice

in Hebrews, where Jeremiah 31 is quoted (8:7-13; 10:12-18). The main teaching of both uses is similar to Jesus' in his institution of communion: Christ inaugurated the new covenant in his sacrificial death (see also Heb. 9:15; cf. 10:20).

There can be no argument that the new covenant benefits of this sacrificial death are designed only for ethnic, national Israel. By linking the new covenant promise with the death of Christ, the NT indicates that the new covenant recipients are the members of Christ's church, both Jew and Gentile.

If this is the case, then when the OT states that the new covenant is made with Israel, the Jews, or the house of Jacob, it does not refer to ethnic, national Israel. It refers rather to the New Israel, the multinational, multiracial church of Jesus Christ.

The NT teaching of the new covenant ("New Testament" really means "New Covenant") therefore delivers a death blow to dispensationalism. For if the recipients of the new covenant which in the OT are identified as Israel are in the NT shown to be converted Jews and Gentiles in the church, we can be certain that there is no distinction between Israel and the church in God's plan. The new covenant church has replaced old covenant Israel in the plan of God. Thus, what Ryrie calls "the essence of dispensationalism" is a mistake, and the theological system is incorrect.

4. The NT teaches that the rebuilding of David's tabernacle is fulfilled in this age in the full inclusion of the Gentiles in God's covenant plan (Ac. 15:13-21; Amos 9:11, 12)[22]

Acts 15 records the events of the so-called Jerusalem council. It was convened for one reason: to answer the vexing "Gentile Question." As noted several times above, Gentiles in the OT were permitted to become the covenant people of God only if they became Jewish, *i.e.*, circumcision for all males.

With the Christian ministry to the Gentiles after Christ's

ascension, especially Paul's, the question naturally arose about a change in God's dealings. In particular, was it any longer necessary for Gentiles to be circumcised if they were to be covenant members, and to keep the Jewish rites (vv. 1-5)?

Peter had earlier been informed by a divine vision (Ac. 10) that the message of salvation in Christ was to include Gentiles without their having to become Jews. He related to the council that there is now "no difference between us [Jews] and them [Gentiles]" (Ac. 15:9).

After Paul and Barnabas informed the council of God's great redemptive work among the Gentiles they had observed in their evangelistic travels, James, seemingly a spokesman, gave his verdict: no longer would Gentiles be required to become Jews (and be circumcised) in order to be included among the covenant people of God. While they should avoid specifically offensive violations of God's law (v. 20), they should not be required to be circumcised or submit to particularly Jewish old covenant rites.

In the course of this answer, James cites Amos 9:11, 12, which promises a rebuilding of "David's tabernacle [house]" (a metaphor for the Judaic kingdom pledged to David [2 Sam. 7:16], and for Israel as whole [Ac. 15:14]) after God has "sift[ed] the house of Israel among the nations" for her sins [Am. 9:9]). A benefit of this Jewish rebuilding is the possession of "the remnant of Edom" (Esau's descendants, Israel's frequent enemies).

When James cites or paraphrases this verse in Acts 15:17, he substitutes "Gentiles" for Edom, and interprets the verse to mean that the rebuilding of David's house would cause the Gentiles to seek the Lord. Thus, to James's way of thinking, the rebuilding of David's tabernacle which was occurring right before their eyes in the apostolic age was drawing into the Christian fold numerous Gentiles, just as Amos had predicted.

Note carefully: At the same time God was turning away

from ethnic Israel as a nation (Ac. 13:44-52) he was rebuilding David's tabernacle, one chief benefit of which was the calling and conversion of a multitude of Gentiles. *God was dismantling the physical house of David precisely while he was rebuilding the true house of David.*

The Davidic covenant is fulfilled in the new covenant church. But if it is the case that the rebuilding of David's tabernacle — that is, the royal lineage of David and the predominance of Israel in general — is fulfilled in the new covenant church at the same time God is suspending his dealings with an unbelieving and rebellious national Israel, the new covenant church must have become the replacement of national, ethnic Israel, the new True Israel, entitled to all the promises (and subject to all the punishments[23]) of old covenant ethnic Israel.

And if this is the case, dispensationalism, whose essence is the distinction between ethnic Israel and the new covenant church, simply cannot be true.

5. The NT calls believing Gentiles true Jews (Rom. 2:28, 29, 9:6-9, 22-30; Gal. 6:15, 16)

The most obvious evidence that the new covenant church has replaced old covenant Israel as the people of God appears in those passages where members of the church (of whatever race) are identified as true Jews.

We've already seen that in John 8:39, 40 Jesus informed the Pharisees that they weren't Abraham's seed since they didn't "do the works of Abraham." The implication is that those who do the works of Abraham are the *actual* seed of Abraham. Does this refer only to believing Jews? Not according to Paul.

In Romans 2:24-29 he reprimands the unconverted Jews for their sin and hypocrisy. They were trusting in their physical lineage as Jews and their imperfect law-keeping (and therefore law-breaking [Rom. 2:1]) rather than in Christ. He rebukes them with the teaching that if Gentiles ("the uncircumcision") keep the law, they're nonetheless considered circumcised (that is, true, godly Jews, God's covenant people), whereas if the ethnic Jews break the law, their circumcision will count for nothing: they will be judged as uncircumcised and unconverted: "[f]or he is not a Jew, which is one outwardly; neither is that circumcision, which is outward in the flesh. But he is a Jew which is one inwardly; and the circumcision is that of the heart…" (vv. 28, 29).

This sounds a great deal like the provisions of the new covenant mentioned above, in which God promised to insert a new, believing heart into his covenant people Israel, that is, all who trust in Christ. The true Jews are those whose heart is right in the sight of God.

This point could not be plainer than in Paul's statements later in Romans (9:6b-8, 24, 25). His teaching is that the word of God in its covenant promises (v. 4) is not ineffectual, even though the majority of the ethnic Jews had abandoned the covenant in unbelief. To replace them, God has raised up new "vessels of mercy" (vv.23-30):

> *For they are not all Israel, which are of Israel: Neither, because they are the seed of Abraham, are they all children: but, in Isaac, shall thy seed be called [Gen. 21:12]. That is, They which are the children of the flesh [that is, ethnic Jews], these are not the children of God: but the children of the promise [all Christians without ethnic distinction] are counted for the seed. (Rom. 9:6b-8)*

Why is the Gentile seed traced through Isaac, even though he was the physical seed of Abraham? Because he was the seed "of promise," a supernaturally given seed, rather than

Ishmael, a merely natural, fleshly seed (Gal. 4:23f.). *God is showing that mere physical lineage is not enough.* The supernatural must transcend (but not eliminate) the natural in God's redemptive plan.

Does this mean individuals in physical Israel are automatically excluded from God's covenant plan? Obviously not, since God's plan is to include both converted Jew and Gentile in his church (Rom. 11:25-32). God wants us to understand that what is vital is not the seed of the flesh, but the seed of promise.[24] The seed of promise is the True Israel, the genuine Jews.

Similarly, in Romans 9:24-29 Paul cites the OT four times (Hos. 1:10; 2:23; Is. 10:22, 13:19) to prove that God's covenantal and redemptive plan has not been thwarted by physical Israel's unbelief. All who trust in Christ alone (Rom. 9:30-10:5), those therefore constituting the new covenant church, have replaced unbelieving, rebellious old covenant ethnic Israel as the obedient, new covenant, True Israel. It is called the "Israel of God" in Galatians 6:15, 16, where it cannot refer only to believing Jews, since the message of vv. 12-15 is that Jewish circumcision is no longer necessary as a mark of covenant inclusion: what is important now is "a new creature [or creation]," one united to Christ by faith (2 Cor. 5:17).

The "Israel of God" includes all those who have become new creatures in Christ. The new covenant church is the New Israel.

CONCLUSION

The objective of this chapter has not been to refute every major tenet of dispensationalism; that would have required an entire book. Rather, I have tried to show that what Charles Ryrie calls "the essence of dispensationalism," the distinction in God's plan between national, ethnic Israel and the new covenant, multiracial church, cannot be sustained when we read the OT in light of the NT.

If we allow the Bible to interpret itself, the bottom line of dispensationalism is faulty; and since the bottom line is faulty, dispensationalism is defective.

CHAPTER 2
THE PROBLEM OF PREMILLENNIALISM

WHEN I USE THE TERM "PREMILLENNIALISM," I refer exclusively to *nondispensational* (or historic) premillennialism.[1] All dispensationalists are premillennialists, but historic premillennialists are not dispensationalists. Historic premillennialists usually recognize the main truth expressed in chapter 1: the new covenant church has replaced (or joined) old covenant Israel as God's covenant people; thus historic premillennialists cannot be dispensational. But they are led by a certain understanding of Revelation 20 to affirm that Christ will return to earth *before* a time of pervasive, divinely enforced peace, the *millennium,* on earth. Indeed, they hold that Christ's coming initiates the millennium. They believe that at the conclusion of the millennium (which may or may not endure an actual 1000 years), Christ will institute the final judgment, separate the unconverted from Christians, and usher in the eternal state. No other passage in Scripture expresses such a course of the future, but premillennialists are convinced that this is just what Revelation 20 teaches.

A SUMMARY OF THE PREMILLENNIAL VIEW

Premillennialism rests chiefly on an interpretation of Revelation 20:5, 6.[2] For this reason, the present chapter will be much shorter than chapter 1. If we can show why the premillennial interpretation of Revelation 20 is flawed, we can refute (historic) premillennialism.

Revelation 20 is the chapter from which the term *millennium* originates. It's not actually found in the chapter, but the expression "thousand years" appears six times. This is designated the "millennium." During this time, Satan is chained and can no longer deceive the nations, and the Christian martyrs who had refused to worship the beast (however that term may be understood) reign with Christ (vv. 3, 4).

Verses 5 and 6 speak of a first resurrection, therefore implying more than one resurrection, just as v. 6 speaks of a second death, thus implying a first death.

Premillennialists assert that the most natural way to read v. 5 is to assume that since the implied second resurrection is indisputably a physical resurrection at the conclusion of the millennium, the explicit first resurrection also must be a physical resurrection — the resurrection of the redeemed, who "live and reign" with Christ on earth.

The fundamental question on which premillennialism rests is whether the first resurrection is a literal resurrection. If it is literal, then the martyrs are resurrected and reign with Christ during the millennium (on earth, premillennialists assume).

At the conclusion of the millennium, the "rest of the dead" (v. 5), *i.e.,* presumably all the unconverted, are resurrected. They then, according to premillennialists, are judged and suffer the "second death" (v. 6), judgment in hell (vv. 14, 15), while Christians enter the bliss of the eternal state.

THE PREMILLENNIAL PROBLEM

The first thing to notice is that there is no express declaration in the passage that Christ will reign physically on earth as premillennialists suppose; as we will see clearly in chapter 4, Christ is presently reigning in heaven, and there is no good reason to assume the kingdom reign mentioned in chapter 20 is not a part of this heavenly throne from which Christ rules the earth.

Revelation chapter 19, which is variously interpreted, depicts Christ riding on a white horse accompanied with heaven's hosts making war on the earthly nations (v. 11-21), but there is no intimation of an earthly, physical reign. This is a passage about judgment, not an earthly, physical reign. Thus, even if Revelation 20:5 denotes a physical resurrection, the passage does not require an earthly, physical reign of Christ such as premillennialists teach.

However, it is hard to imagine a wholesale physical resurrection apart from the Second Advent, and on this point the premillennialists are quite correct. They are only wrong to suggest **two** physical resurrections separated by the millennium. The fact is that *regeneration* is pointedly and metaphorically equated with resurrection in the Bible (Jn. 11:25, 26; Eph. 2:1-6). Not only so, but in John 5:25-29, the spiritual resurrection of regeneration is discussed (as it is in Rev. 20) in the very context of the physical resurrection. The dead to whom the Father and Son give life **now** "live" *spiritually* (v. 25).[3]

Subsequently, both the good and evil will be resurrected from the grave *physically* and enter the eternal state (vv. 28-29). In the light of the rest of the Bible, the best way to understand the "first resurrection" of Revelation 20 is to see it as *the spiritual resurrection of regeneration in any age*.

In all passages besides Revelation 20 which refer to the resurrection, it is identified as a single event at which both saved and lost are judged. We noted John 5:25-29, but the same is true of John 6:39-54, where the righteous are to be raised up "at the last day."

In 1 Corinthians 15:22, 23 there is no mention of the resurrection of both saved and unsaved as in the Gospel of John and in Revelation but it is plainly stated that the "end" occurs at the coming of Christ. There is no room for a millennium between a physical resurrection for the converted and a separate, physical resurrection for the unconverted.

The problem of premillennialism is the attempt to base an eschatological view on a single text in a highly symbolic book (a fact even dispensationalists recognize[4]), particularly when this view conflicts with the view of clearer biblical passages on the topic.

Postmillennialists (and amillennialists) interpret the first resurrection of Revelation 20:5, 6 as regeneration; the other Scriptures noted above support this. Postmillennialists (and amillennialists) interpret the reign of the martyrs as their present pre-physical-resurrection reign with Christ on his Davidic throne (see chapter 4). This interpretation agrees much more closely with the Bible's teachings that Christ is presently reigning, and that there is only one resurrection of both the just and the unjust at "the end" (1 Cor. 15:24), "the last day" (Jn. 6:39-54).

CONCLUSION

Unlike dispensationalism, premillennialism is not a flagrant misunderstanding of the scheme of the Bible; it is a misunderstanding of a single text.

Unfortunately, it has a greater impact on one's theological views and practices than one would expect from a single text. If we take all the revelation of the Bible into account, we find that the premillennial interpretation of Revelation does not do justice to what the Bible actually teaches.

CHAPTER 3
THE ANOMALY OF AMILLENNIALISM

WHAT IS AMILLENNIALISM?[1] It is the view that Christ instituted the millennium at his First Advent (or sometime between the First and Second Advents), but that the kingdom prophecies of the OT are fulfilled in the church, the deceased saints now in heaven, or the eternal state.

The "a" in *a*millennialism means "no": no millennium. This is not entirely accurate, however. Amillennialists do not really deny the millennium of Revelation 20; they do deny the *type* of millennium premillennialists or postmillennialists support. They deny that there will be any earthly time of godly peace and prosperity either before the Second Advent (as postmillennialists assert) or after the Second Advent (as premillennialists assert).

Amillennialism starts well and ends poorly. It correctly asserts that the NT should interpret the OT: the entire Bible must be the source of eschatological teaching. This, as we saw in chapter 1, is the right way of interpretation. Amillennialism supports the proper interpretive method, *but does not employ it properly*. It does not properly account for the glorious kingdom promises of the OT.

For this reason, we postmillennialists have mixed feelings

about amillennialism. In fact, some theologians argue that postmillennialism is a species of amillennialism. On the one hand, it uses the proper interpretive method; on the other hand, its conclusions from that method are sometimes unsound, especially when dealing with the kingdom promises of the OT. This is the anomaly of amillennialism which this brief chapter will address.

THE OLD TESTAMENT PREDICTS A GODLY GOLDEN AGE ON EARTH

The OT contains numerous prophecies of a godly golden age on the earth during which righteousness and the righteous will flourish. I will mention only several of the most prominent.

In Numbers 14:21, during a tense conversation with Moses, God promises, "But as truly as I live, all the earth shall be filled with the glory of the LORD." God then pledges that the unbelieving Jewish generation that left Egypt will not exert dominion in Canaan, but that he will raise up a believing generation that will trust and obey him. Apparently the godly dominion of Canaan would be a foretaste of a time when the glory of God would engulf the entire earth (see chapter 4).

The Psalms contain a number of predictions of a godly golden age. Psalm 2, for example, prophesies that the Son of the LORD Jehovah will ask his Father for the nations of the earth as his inheritance, and its far reaches as his possession (v. 8). He will strike down and overwhelm all heathen (Gentile) nations.

Psalm 22:27 takes a slightly different tack. It declares, "All the ends of the world shall remember and turn unto the LORD: and all the kindreds of the nations shall worship before thee." Likewise, Psalm 47:2, 3, 7, 8 declare:

> For *the LORD most high is terrible;* **he is a great King over all the earth**. *He shall subdue the people under us, and the nations under our feet,.... For God is the King of* **all the earth**: *sing ye praise with understanding. God reigneth* **over the heathen** *[Gentile nations]: God sitteth upon the throne of his holiness. [emphasis supplied]*

The theme of subduing God's enemies "under his feet" (or similar language) is frequent in Scripture (Ps. 68:23; 91:13; 110:1; Is. 28:3; Mal. 4:2, 3; Ac. 2:35; Rom. 16:20; 1 Cor. 15:25; Eph. 1:22; Heb. 1:13; 2:8); it probably originates in Genesis 3:15, which predicts that the seed of the woman is to crush the head of the seed of the serpent, while the seed of the serpent is to crush the heel of the seed of the woman.[2] In any case, Psalm 47 predicts that God will subdue the nations under the feet of the righteous.

Psalm 72 is perhaps the clearest of the Psalms prophesying the godly golden age, the reign of "the king's son [prophetically of Jesus Christ]" (v. 1): "In his days shall the righteous flourish; and abundance of peace so long as the moon endureth.... [H]is enemies shall lick the dust .... [A]ll kings shall fall down before him: all nations shall serve him" (vv. 7, 9, 11). During this great era there is to be true justice (vv. 2, 4, 12-14) and abundance of provision (v. 16). The kings of the earth will bow to and honor God, his Son, and his people (v. 10). Likewise, Psalm 86:9 predicts that "All nations whom thou [God] has made shall come and worship before thee."

The OT prophets are no less certain of the future godly golden age. Isaiah 2:2-4 envisions a time when the Lord's house will be exalted in the earth. Many nations and peoples will hungrily appeal to "the God of Jacob" and learn of the Lord and his law. War and international conflicts will cease.

Similarly, chapter 11:1-10 speaks glowingly of a day when

a Branch (Christ) will issue from Jesse's root (the lineage of David) and judge the entire earth in righteousness. It will be an era of great domestic peace, and the harmony of nature with man. In fact, "the earth shall be full of the knowledge of the LORD as the waters cover the sea" (v. 9).

Chapter 42:1-4 refers to God's "servant" (Jesus Christ) who will not be thwarted in his task to "set judgment in the earth" until "the isles [Gentile nations] shall wait for his law" (v. 4), and chapter 65:17-25 describes the new heavens and new earth,[3] in which the people of God will no longer weep, life expectancy will be greatly expanded, the godly will eat freely of the fruit of their labor, and nature will again (much like before the Fall) harmonize with man. This cannot refer to the eternal state, since the symbolic discussion of life expectancy, agrarian labor, and nature's increased harmony with man are not appropriate to the eternal state.

Daniel is quite graphic in his description of the soon-to-be-arriving Kingdom of the Messiah (7:13-14, 26–27):

> *I saw in the night visions, and, behold, one like the Son of man **came with the clouds of heaven**, and came to the Ancient of days, and they brought him near before him. **And there was given him dominion, and glory, and a kingdom, that all people, nations, and languages, should serve him**: his dominion is an everlasting dominion, which shall not pass away, and his kingdom that which shall not be destroyed…*
>
> *But the judgment [heavenly court] shall sit, and they shall take away his [an evil earthly ruler's] dominion, to consume and to destroy it unto the end. And the kingdom and dominion, and the greatness of the kingdom under the whole heaven, **shall be given to the people of the saints of the most High**, whose kingdom is an everlasting*

> *kingdom, and all dominions shall serve and obey him. (emphases supplied)*

Daniel sees the Son of Man ascending on the clouds to the heavenly throne of God the Father. This quite clearly is referring to the ascension of our Lord Jesus Christ. The disciples saw him ascend to heaven in the clouds. This is referring not to his *de*scent at the future Second Advent. It refers to his ascent after his First Advent. When Jesus Christ ascended into the heavens to this Father, he ascended to take his throne, ruling over "all people, nations, and languages." And one consequence of that rule from heaven over earth is that his saints were to join him in that reign over the nations (see also Eph. 1:3, 20-23; 2:6).

The prophet Micah (4:1-5) uses language similar to Isaiah to describe a time when God's house will be exalted, the nations will joyously enter it to learn of God and his law, and when God will rule the nations of the earth in justice, assuring worldwide peace and harmony. Portions of these predictions appear also in Zechariah 9:10 and Malachi 1:11.

A clear message of the OT is that there will come a time on earth when God through his Son and people will rule the earth in justice and holiness, producing a worldwide love for himself and his law and a pervasive international peace and great material abundance. This is one of the great hopes of the prophets.

THE NEW TESTAMENT VERIFIES, NOT REVERSES, THE KINGDOM PROMISES

Because amillennialists believe the Bible, they in no way deny the fact of these prophecies. The error of amillennialism, however, is in assuming that all these and other similar OT prophecies will be fulfilled in the church, the deceased presently in heaven, or in the eternal state, and will not overwhelm the world as the Scriptures seem to teach.[4] Amillennialists rightly recognize (as we noted in chapter 1) that the NT must interpret the OT, but they think, that the passages of the NT which supposedly predict widespread evil and apostasy will not permit us to believe that there is to be a godly golden age before Christ's return.[5] The NT interprets the OT promises in a truncated way. But in fact the NT does not permit this limitation but demands, rather, an *expansion* of the promises.

In amillennial thinking, the victorious, symbolic language of the OT must be interpreted mainly to refer to victory in the church or in eternity. Just as the physical redemptive types of the old covenant are replaced by the spiritual redemptive realities of the new covenant (Heb. 8-10), so the physical eschatological predictions of the old covenant are replaced by the spiritual eschatological realities of the new covenant.

We postmillennialists agree with the amillennialists that the NT does not portray the revival of a merely physical kingdom like that over which David and Solomon ruled. We agree that the realities of the kingdom are not limited to or based in time and history. We agree that Christ's kingdom is greater than merely human and physical realities. *But we do not agree that the kingdom no longer pertains to all human life and society.* We hold that it is precisely designed to overwhelm the entire earth (see chapter 4).

The NT universalizes the worship of the OT; it is no longer limited to the temple and the Aaronic priesthood. By virtue of Christ's final, once-for-all atonement as our Great High Priest (Heb. 9), the saints may now worship anywhere without a merely human mediator (Jn. 4:21-24; Heb. 10:1-14). Christ is the mediator of the new covenant, which is not only for Jews in Canaan, but for all people throughout the earth.

For much of the OT, the kingdom of God had a localized form — *i.e.,* in Jerusalem, in conjunction with the temple and the ark of the covenant.

But in the new covenant era, the kingdom of God in Christ is universalized (Heb. 12:24-29); it knows no local limits; it engulfs heaven and earth.

As we will note in chapter 4, the NT in no way interprets the OT kingdom passages promising a godly golden age as fulfilled only in the church or the eternal state. In effect, therefore, amillennialism wants to "re-localize" the kingdom. It wants the glorious kingdom realities pledged by the OT limited to heaven, the church, or the eternal state. The kingdom promises certainly do pertain to these, but they pertain to all the earth in time and history, too.

KINGDOM PROMISES THAT MUST PERTAIN TO THE ENTIRE EARTH

Certain OT passages predicting the kingdom glories, even given their symbolic character, simply cannot be limited to the church or the eternal state. The entire earth, not just the church, is to bow to our Savior-King, the Lord Jesus Christ.

God's righteous rule extends to **the whole earth** (Ps. 47:2; 97:5). As we saw above in Psalm 22:27; 47:2-8; 72; and 86:9, the Kingship of God and his anointed extends to **the whole earth**, including to earthly kings and Gentile nations far from Jerusalem. This kingship, we noted, secures earthly righteousness and peace, a godly golden age. It cannot be tapered to the church or the eternal state.

While Isaiah 2:2-4 may be construed to refer only to the eternal state (though we postmillennialists believe it does not), chapter 11:1-10 must refer to the godly golden age in the earth: "[T]he earth shall be full of the knowledge of the LORD as the waters cover the sea" (v. 9). This makes no sense if it refers only to the eternal state. For instance, the prediction that the Messiah will smite the earth with the rod of his mouth (v. 4) finds fulfillment not in the Revelation 20 millennium, but the Revelation 19 Great Commission (see v. 15).[6]

And verses 11–16 refer to God's work in history with the Gentile nations and cannot denote the eternal state.

Similarly, the great, righteous kingdom predicted in Isaiah 42:1-4 cannot pertain to the eternal state. The other passages noted above which refer to earthly peace, prosperity and justice make no sense if limited to the church or to the eternal state (to bring up even the possibility of conflict, poverty, or injustice in eternity is impertinent).

The OT does not imply that the kingdom promises are to be realized *only* in the church or the eternal state; and the NT does not alter the scope of those promises.

The NT teaches that the new covenant church has replaced old covenant Israel (see chapter 1); it does *not* teach that eternal, heavenly promises have replaced temporal, earthly promises. The chief hope of God's people is their heavenly hope joined to a resurrected earth (Tit. 2:13; Rev. 21:1–3). This was just as true of OT saints as it is of Christians today (Heb. 11:13-16). This does not mean that Christians have no earthly hope. Chapter 4 will document this.

CONCLUSION

The anomaly of amillennialism is that although it has the right *approach* to interpreting the kingdom promises (the NT must interpret the OT), it does not take account of the worldwide scope of the kingdom promises. Chapter 4 will show that the NT verifies the worldwide scope of the OT kingdom promises, and assures, in addition, the power of Christ and the Holy Spirit to accomplish the advancement of Christ's comprehensive kingdom.

CHAPTER 4
THE PROMISE OF POSTMILLENNIALISM

IN SOME WAYS THE EXPRESSION "POSTMILLENNIALISM," like "amillennialism," does not accurately describe the view it designates. While postmillennialists do hold that Christ will return after the earthly millennium, their position does not rest chiefly on their interpretation of the millennium mentioned in Revelation 20 as premillennialism's does.

The argument for postmillennialism, rather, derives from those passages that promise (1) a great extended era of earthly righteousness, peace, and prosperity; (2) the incremental advancement of God's and Christ's kingdom in human history during the interadvental era (the period between the First and Second Advents); and (3) the unique and potent presence of God accompanying and energizing his covenant people in their kingdom-advancing commission.

It must be made clear that the exact timing of the millennium in relation to the Second Advent is not a main theme of postmillennialists. Unlike dispensationalists and many other premillennialists, postmillennialists are not obsessed with the precise timing of the millennium in relation to the Second Advent, *but are concerned with Christ's advancing kingdom in time and history.* The argument for postmillennialism issues chiefly from those glorious, precious promises of the gradual but relentless progress of Christ's kingdom resulting from the ministry of his *First* Advent. This evidence is summarized in the remainder of this chapter.

PASSAGES THAT PROMISE A GREAT, EXTENDED ERA OF EARTHLY PEACE, PROSPERITY AND HOLINESS

We have observed in chapter 3 (and thus won't rehearse here) those OT passages that promise a godly golden age which amillennialists do not believe can apply to the entire earth. There is no question that in numerous places God in the OT promises a time of glorious peace, abundant prosperity, and global righteousness. The only question is, what is the nature of those promises, how will they be fulfilled, and *when* will they be fulfilled?

We have noted that premillennialists err in assuming they cannot be fulfilled until the Second Advent (premillennialists identify the OT kingdom promises with the millennium of Revelation 20).

We have noted, further, that amillennialists err in limiting the scope of those kingdom prophecies to the church, the deceased saints in heaven, or the eternal state.

In chapter 1 we observed that the NT interpretation of the OT will not permit dispensational conclusions; in this chapter we will note that the NT usage of the OT demands postmillennial conclusions: (1) That the millennium occurs in the interadvental era and (2) that the kingdom of God will advance gradually, both in intensity and extent, during human history.

PASSAGES THAT PROMISE THE INCREMENTAL ADVANCEMENT OF GOD'S AND CHRIST'S KINGDOM IN HUMAN HISTORY

1. God has promised that the seed of Abraham will inherit the earth (Gen. 17:7, 8; 22:15-18; Rom. 4:13; Gal. 3:29)

We noted in chapter 1 that the Abrahamic covenant is a present reality in the new covenant era. The promises of the Abrahamic covenant are the possession of today's Christians. One of those promises is Israel's possession of the land of Canaan and the defeat of her enemies.

Are we new covenant Christians therefore entitled to the land of Canaan and the defeat of Israel's enemies? Yes, but we are entitled to (and responsible for) much more than this, and in a much more comprehensive way.

When Paul refers in Romans 4:13 to the land promises and blessing promises of the Abrahamic covenant, he extends them to include not just Canaan, but the *entire earth*: Abraham and his seed are to be "heir of the world." This is not quite how the OT framed the land promises, or the blessing promises. There the land promises pertain essentially to Canaan, known as the "Promised Land"; and the blessing promises simply state that the seed of Abraham will bless the nations of the earth.

Paul, however, interprets this promise more broadly. This is just one more case of the NT interpreting the OT. Just as the new covenant expands the people of God to include a worldwide race of the redeemed, so it expands the land promises of the Abrahamic covenant to include the entire earth. The whole earth is the promised possession of the new covenant people of God. John Murray states:

> The clause "that he should be heir of the world" is explanatory of the promise given to Abraham and his seed; it tells us what the promise was. We do not find any promise in the Old

> Testament in these express terms. What is it? We naturally think of the promise to Abraham that in him all the families of the earth would be blessed (*cf.* Gen. 13:14-17; 15:4, 5, 18-21; 17:2-21; 22:15-18). In light of Pauline teaching as a whole, however, we cannot exclude from the scope of this promise, as defined by the apostle, the most inclusive messianic purport. It is defined as the promise to Abraham that *he* should be heir of the world, but it is also a promise to his seed and, therefore, can hardly involve anything less than the **worldwide dominion promised to Christ** and to the spiritual seed of Abraham in him. It is a promise that receives its ultimate fulfillment in the consummated order of the new heavens and the new earth.[1]

It is true that the "ultimate fulfillment" of the Abrahamic covenant will not occur until the eternal state; but, as Murray implies, "worldwide dominion" begins with Christ and Christians in the present new covenant era. The promises to the old covenant Jews of dominion in Canaan are *expanded* in the NT to include the entire earth, which is the possession not of ethnic Jews but of True Israel, the Christian church.

We will see in section 3 that the promise of the defeat of Israel's (and therefore God's) enemies is fulfilled by Christ in this new covenant age. The multinational, worldwide, new covenant Israel (the Christian church) has replaced ethnic old covenant Israel. Similarly, *the worldwide dominion commission has replaced the Palestinian dominion commission.*

Abraham's seed is a present reality in the interadvental era. We saw in chapter 1 that all united to Christ by faith in the present age are the seed of Abraham and heirs of the Abrahamic covenantal promises. We noted the four chief promises: a relationship (God would be God in a special sense to Abraham), a seed (God would be a God in a special sense to Abraham's vast posterity), a land (Canaan), and a blessing (to the other nations).

It is important to note that the same God who promised he would be a God to Abraham and his seed (which the NT identifies as Christ and all united to him by faith) also promised that the seed would bless the nations and inherit the land. The nations are blessed in Christ, who bursts asunder the OT limitation of the covenant to ethnic Jews and now calls his people from every nation under heaven (Eph. 2:11-22; Rev. 7:9, 10).

In addition, these Christians from every nation are now heirs (with Christ, Rom. 8:17) of the entire earth (Rom. 4:13). We cannot say that only certain of the promises given to Christ as Abraham's seed are realized by the new covenant community in the present era, and that after the Second Coming, the other promises are realized. We might say that all the promises are only partially realized now, and will be realized in their *fullness* only in eternity; but we cannot say that any of the promises of the Abrahamic covenant are not presently given to the seed of Abraham, those united to Christ by faith.

A pledge to Abraham in Genesis 22:15-18 is that his seed will possess the gate of their enemies, possibly prefiguring Matthew 16:18, which asserts that the gates of Hell (Hades) will not prevail against Christ's church. The language is symbolic. The gates of the city are identified with its power, the seat of its authority (Pr. 31:23; Jer. 14:2, 3). To possess the gates of the city is therefore to possess and control the city. The promise to Abraham's seed secures the vanquishing of Israel's enemies.

From the NT, recall, we discover that Christians are the seed of Abraham, the True Israel. They are heirs of the promises of the Abrahamic covenant (Gal. 3:29). One of the promises is the land promise, expanded in the NT to include the entire world. This requires the subordination of Christ's enemies (1 Cor. 15:24, 25); it is exactly what Genesis 22 predicted: the seed of Abraham will possess the gates of her enemies. This can hardly require less than the worldwide dominion of Christ and his elect, the re-establishment of Christian civilization and Christian culture.

2. God has promised that Christ's kingdom will overwhelm the earth (Dan. 2:31f.).

Daniel 2 records his interpretation of Nebuchadnezzar's dream about the great image. It is perhaps the most persuasive point favoring postmillennialism in the OT. Much of the revelation to Daniel, like that given to John in the Book of Revelation, is symbolic. Our intent here is not to offer an interpretation of the entire book, or even the entire chapter. Instead, it is to show how chapter 2:31f. supports the postmillennial view.

The image of Nebuchadnezzar's dream refers to four similar historical kingdoms which ruled successively. Most historical scholars are agreed[2] that the four kingdoms are the four great ancient world empires: the head of the image made of fine gold is Babylon; the image's silver breast and arms picture the Medes and Persians; Greece is likened to the brass belly and thighs; and the Roman Empire is typified by the iron and clay legs and feet, a mixture of strength and weakness (Dan. 2:42, 43). A small "stone... cut out without hands [supernaturally hurled]" (v. 34) smashes the image on the feet (the Roman Empire) and thereby destroys the image. The small stone then grows and becomes a mountain that fills the entire earth (vv. 34, 35). Daniel's interpretation of v. 44 clinches the postmillennial argument:

> *And in the days of these kings shall the God of*
> *heaven set up a kingdom, which shall never be*
> *destroyed: and the kingdom shall not be left to*
> *other people [as the other four kingdoms were],*
> *but it shall break in pieces and consume all these*

> *kingdoms, and it [unlike the other four empires]*
> *shall stand forever.*

The expression "In the days of these kings" clinches the postmillennial argument. The everlasting kingdom God was to establish in the earth begins when the stone collides with the image's feet (the Roman Empire), consumes all the ancient empires of which Rome was the final installment, and subsequently overwhelms the earth. That is, *during the Roman Empire God launched his final, impregnable kingdom in the earth.*

When was this? It could be only during the period of Christ's earthly ministry and resurrection and session at the Father's right hand (see 3 below). Christ claimed to be setting up a kingdom at his First Advent (Mt. 4:17, 23; 12:27-29). This is the everlasting kingdom of which Daniel spoke. This is the kingdom the apostles preached (Ac. 8:12; 20:25, 28:23, 31). It is the kingdom which finally toppled the pagan Roman Empire in A.D. 312 with Constantine's conversion.

Note carefully: the everlasting kingdom predicted by God through Daniel is not established at Christ's Second Advent, but at his First Advent. "[I]n the days of these kings"— not the 21st century.

The reign of Revelation 20, therefore, is not a reign of Christ physically on earth in the near or distant future (recall that Revelation 20 says nothing about Christ reigning on earth). The reign of Revelation 20 is the same heaven-over-earth reign as Daniel 2: the present reign of Christ established at his first Advent.

If there is any question about the timing of that reign, we may consider as we did on chapter 3 the night vision of Daniel recorded in 7:13, 14. Again, our purpose is not to detail the historic occasion and entire interpretation of the vision. Rather, it is to note that when the Son of Man (Christ, Mt. 16:13) "came" with the clouds of heaven, he was brought to the Ancient of days (God Almighty; see Dan. 7:9, 22), and given a worldwide dominion.

It is hard to imagine anyone's not recognizing the clouds of heaven as a reference to Christ's ascension (Ac. 1:9). Further, the main time Christ was absent from his place with the Father (Phil. 2:5-8) is during his earthly ministry (there are no recorded Christophanies [pre-incarnate appearances of Christ] after the book of Daniel). The only time Christ ever returned gloriously and triumphantly to the Ancient of Days was when he returned to heaven from his earthly ministry. This is when he was escorted back to the Father's throne and formally granted his everlasting kingdom. The most obvious understanding of Daniel 7:13, 14 is that Christ received his kingdom immediately following his ascension.

This kingdom established at Christ's First Advent and formally recognized and bestowed at his ascension is the kingdom that Daniel predicts will overwhelm the earth.

3. The NT teaches that Christ's enthronement mentioned in Psalm 110:1 is instituted and/or fulfilled in the present age (Ac. 2:29-36; Eph. 1:20-22; 1 Cor. 15:27; Heb. 10:12-14)[3]

Another decisive biblical teaching supporting postmillennialism is the NT teaching which links the enthronement passage of Psalm 110 with Christ's present rule. Psalm 110 predicts the conversion or destruction (or destruction by conversion) of the heathen and Christ's other enemies as a reward to the LORD's [Jehovah's] Lord [Christ]. The image used is similar to that of Genesis 3:15 noted above: the enemies are to be made Christ's "footstool." Likewise, the scope of the promise recalls Genesis 3:15 about the crushing of the head of the serpent's seed: "He shall wound the heads of many countries" (Ps. 110:6). This is a remarkable, all-embracing prediction.

When we come to the NT, we discover in Luke 1:26-33,

Acts 2:29-36, 1 Corinthians 15:27, Ephesians 1:20, and Hebrews 10:12-14, that this OT passage refers to Christ's present reign — not in some future millennial era after the Second Advent, but in the interadvental era as a result of his victorious death, resurrection, ascension, and present session at the right hand of God.

It is clear from Peter's Pentecostal sermon in Acts 2 that when David spoke in Psalm 110 of the conquering son of Jehovah (vv. 34, 35) and in Psalm 16 of resurrection (vv. 2:25-28), he was predicting the present reign of Christ. It would have been senseless for Peter to have introduced Psalm 110 as fulfilled in the interadvental age as a result of the effect of Christ's death, resurrection, ascension, and session if what Peter had *really* meant to say was that the glorious reign and defeat of God's enemies which Psalm 110 portrays is not designed to occur until the Second Advent. Peter teaches that Christ's rule predicted in Psalm 110 is operative in the present age.

Perhaps no passage in the NT is more crucial to determining the relation between Christ's kingdom and his Second Advent, however, than 1 Corinthians 15:22-25:

> *For as in Adam all die, even so in Christ shall all be made alive. But every man in his own order: Christ the firstfruits; afterward they that are Christ's at his coming. Then cometh the end, when he shall have delivered up the kingdom to God, even the Father; when he shall have put down all rule and all authority and power; For he must reign, till he hath put all enemies under his feet.*

The topic of 1 Corinthians 15 is the resurrection. Christ is the "firstfruits," the first of many to come after, that is, all deceased Christians who will be physically resurrected at the

Second Advent. Significantly, "then cometh the end" — not the millennium, which will have been past — after Christ has subjugated all hostile powers on earth.

Paul quotes or alludes to Psalm 110 in declaring that the end of time occurs when Christ returns to earth, after he has "put down all rule and all authority and power."

This is the express truth of Romans 14:9, "For to this end Christ both died, and rose, that he might be Lord both of the dead and living." He rose from the grave in victory to rule the earth from heaven. The "end" occurs when Christ returns, after he has "put down" his enemies. *He will not return to earth until all his enemies (except death itself) have been made his footstool.* Christ will conquer his enemies from his heavenly throne, then return to earth to initiate the final judgment and the eternal state. 1 Corinthians 15:22-25 therefore cites or refers to Psalm 110 as proof of Christ's present reign and progressive subordination of his enemies.

Likewise, Paul in Ephesians 1:20-22 quotes Psalm 110:1 in linking Christ's present reign with his resurrection. God has "raised [Christ] from the dead, and set him at his own right hand in the heavenly places," where he rules "[f]ar above all principality, and power, and might, and dominion, and every name that is named, not only in this world, but also in that which is to come: [a]nd hath put all things under his feet." This glorious present reign is the gracious inheritance of Christians today (vv. 18, 19); it is not postponed until the Second Advent. As in 1 Corinthians 15:22-25, Paul teaches that the reign of Christ began in earnest after the resurrection; it seems, in fact, that the resurrection paved the way for the formal institution of his heavenly coronation. Psalm 110:1 is the OT foundation of Paul's argument that Christ presently reigns at the right hand of the Father, waiting until his enemies are placed "under his feet."

Similarly, in Hebrews 10:12-13 the biblical writer cites Psalm 110:1 but appropriates the reference to Christ.

Hebrews, however, is concerned mostly with the finality of Christ's redemptive ministry, not with his resurrection. One aspect of that ministry is the reign to which he is entitled as a result of it:

> *But this man, after he had offered one sacrifice for sins forever, sat down on the right hand of God; From henceforth expecting till his enemies be made his footstool.*

The writer quotes Psalm 110:1 to support his statement that by virtue of Christ's substitutionary atonement he is risen to regal glory beside the Father, by whom all his enemies will be subjugated. Christ is the One under whose feet God has placed all things. There is no hint that it is Christ's Second Advent that initiates his reign over the earth; rather, it is his death at his **First** Advent that institutes that reign. The promise of Psalm 110 that Christ will reign over the earth and subordinate his enemies is fulfilled in the present age as a result of Christ's death and resurrection, not in a future age as a result of his Second Advent.

A related passage is Luke 1:26-33, in which we discover that in the angel Gabriel's visit to Mary, the mother of Jesus, he assures her that "the Lord God will give unto him [Jesus Christ] the throne of his father David: and he shall reign over the house of Jacob forever; and of his kingdom there shall be no end" (vv. 32–33).

This refers to the promises of the Davidic covenant (2 Sam. 7) discussed in chapter 1 — God would preserve David's seed on Israel's throne. Isaiah 9:7, Ezekiel 37:24, 25, and Hosea 3:5 all powerfully verify this divine pledge.

As we noted in chapter 1, Acts 15:15-17 teaches that the Davidic covenant is fulfilled in the present interadvental age. When Gabriel announced God's intention for Mary's critical role in the incarnation, he was equally assuring her that the royal seed of David to whom the OT pointed was *Christ*. He would establish during his first Advent his benevolent but comprehensive and irrepressible rule in the earth.

All this is especially hard for dispensationalists and many premillennialists to grasp or accept, since they equate the promises of Psalm 110 and the Davidic throne in 2 Samuel 7 and elsewhere with a future restored Jewish kingdom on earth after the Second Advent. *It is another example of not letting the NT interpret the OT.*

If we read just the OT, we would get the distinct impression that the kingdom over which Jehovah's Son was to rule is the earthly Jerusalem, by which his reign could extend to the entire earth. We would assume that the enemies he would defeat will be ethnic Israel's enemies, whom he identifies as his own. We would likely conclude that all the nations will travel to Jerusalem in Israel to learn of God and his law. *But we would be wrong.* The NT interprets the kingdom promises. And when it does, it declares that Jehovah's Son is Jesus (Mt. 22:41-45); that he reigns *now* at his Father's right hand (Heb. 10:12-13); that the enemies he defeats are the church's enemies throughout the earth (Eph. 1:20-23); and that Jerusalem is not the earthly Jerusalem, but the heavenly Jerusalem of God's church, God's elect in the earth (Heb. 12:22, 23).

God predicts that he will put all enemies under Christ's feet as the result of Christ's crucifixion, resurrection, ascension, and present session at the Father's right hand. He will not postpone placing his enemies under Christ's feet until the Second Advent. 1 Corinthians 15:23, 24 is clear: when Christ returns to earth, then comes *the end*. The kingdom will have been delivered up to the Father at the end of time, that is, the time of Christ's coming. The OT promises of Messiah's reign are fulfilled in the present interadvental age.

Therefore, the kingdom of God and of Christ is a *present* reality in the earth. God is *presently* subordinating his enemies to his Son's kingdom reign. In *this*, the interadvental era, he is relentlessly advancing his kingdom.

4. God has promised that Christ's kingdom will advance gradually (Mt. 13:31-33; Heb. 2:8)

A principal argument against postmillennialism is that we moderns do not see Christ's kingdom advancing before our eyes, but that, as a matter of fact, the world is becoming increasingly evil. This is untrue on both counts,[4] but the main point here is that the Bible does not require an immediate perception the kingdom's advancement by unaided human eyes. In fact, it requires almost the contrary.

Among the kingdom parables of Matthew 13 appear two (vv. 31-33) that describe the pace of kingdom advancement. The parable of the mustard seed expresses the lesson that the kingdom of God begins minutely and grows to benefit the entire earth. The parable of the yeast expresses the lesson that the kingdom begins as a tiny force but eventually influences the entire earth.

These two parables emphasize three crucial truths about the kingdom of God: (1) it has a small beginning; (2) it grows gradually; and (3) it eventually becomes massive. The kingdom of God does not begin with a great external, public cataclysm as most premillennialists hold; rather, it began humbly at Christ's *First* Advent (Mt. 2:1-12; Lk. 1:30-33; 2:8-17). It is not accomplished all at once. It slowly and gradually overwhelms the earth. This teaching is strikingly similar to that of Daniel 2:35, 44, 45 that the everlasting kingdom God establishes during the Roman Empire vanquishes that empire and grows relentlessly to overspread and dominate the earth.

If this is so, why is there such evil in the world? If Christ is presently reigning at his Father's right hand, why do we not see more evidence of that reign in the earth? The Bible offers the clear answer. Hebrews 2:8 cites Psalm 110:1 in expressing that God has put all things (in the present age) under Christ's feet. It goes on to say, notably, that "we see not yet all things put under him." In other words, and bearing in mind the teaching of Daniel 2 and the kingdom parables of Matthew 13, the kingdom's growth is gradual; we do not observe its effects immediately. The kingdom has been established definitively but must work its way out in history. We do not yet see all things placed under Christ's feet, but the fact that we do not see this does not mean that the kingdom is not present.

As Calvin explains: "As Christ carries on war continually with various enemies, it is doubtless evident that he has no quiet possession of his kingdom. He is not, however, under necessity of waging war; but it happens through his will that his enemies are not to be subdued till the last day, in order that we may be tried and proved by fresh experiences."[5]

Had he wanted, God could have crushed Christ's enemies at any time. His will, however, is that his people be faithful in advancing his cause and kingdom. Little by little his enemies are vanquished (by salvation or judgment), and his kingdom extends throughout the earth.

PASSAGES THAT PROMISE THE UNIQUE AND POTENT PRESENCE OF GOD ACCOMPANYING AND ENERGIZING HIS COVENANT PEOPLE IN THEIR KINGDOM-ADVANCING COMMISSION

Not only does the Bible teach that Christ's kingdom will advance in the present interadvental period; it also teaches that God has undertaken to energize this covenant body to perform this task. Daniel 7:27 promises "[t]he kingdom and dominion, and the greatness of the kingdom under the whole heaven, shall be given to the people of the saints of the most High, whose kingdom is an everlasting kingdom, and all dominions shall serve and obey him." The saints of God are charged with possessing and maintaining Christ's kingdom

(Rev. 2:26, 27). It almost goes without saying that God has equipped and energized them for this task.

An obvious example is Matthew 16:18, in which Christ pledges that the gates of Hades will not prevail against his church. As mentioned above, this may hark back to the prediction of Genesis 22:17 that Abraham's seed would possess the gates of her enemies.

It is critical to recognize that gates are not offensive weapons; the picture in Matthew 16:18 is not one of Christ's church "holding the fort" until Christ rescues the church from Satan's clutching grasp, *but of the inability of Satan's deathly stronghold to resist the onslaught of the advancing army of Christ's church.* The gates of Hell cannot repel Christ's church in its earthly advance.

Matthew 28:18-20 teaches the same thing in a different way. This "Great Commission" is that the Christians are to disciple and baptize all nations, with the assurance that Christ will accompany them until the end of the age. This is a comprehensive calling; it requires not just individual salvation, but the *discipling of the nations.*

To baptize the nations is to bring them under Christ's authority, since baptism is a covenantal sign and seal binding the Triune God to the believer and the believer to the Triune God.[6] Baptism is the initial external mark of the covenant (communion is the continuing external mark). To baptize is to begin the external work of disciple-making. Christ has commissioned his church to bring all nations under his authority.[7] Christ promises that he will accompany his church in this world-conquering task until that task is complete at the end of the age.

Not long before his ascension, moreover, Christ in John 16:7-12 informed his discouraged disciples that it was necessary for him to return to heaven so that the Holy Spirit, who should reprove the world, would arrive to accomplish God's redemptive purposes in the earth. In chapter 14:12 Jesus promises, "He that believeth on me, the works that I do he shall do also; and greater works than these shall he do; because I go unto my Father."

Christ's teaching was not that his work was more effective when he was (or is) on earth, but rather *when he returned to heaven*. There, as we have noted, he was formally enthroned on the Father's right hand, and dispatched his Spirit to his church on earth (Ac. 2:30-33). He dispatched his Spirit to energize his people in their task to disciple the nations, exerting dominion in the earth under his regal authority.

CONCLUSION

The evidence of the Bible supports the postmillennial perspective. The Bible promises (1) a great, extended era of earthly righteousness, peace, and prosperity; (2) the gradual but real advancement of Christ's kingdom in human history during the interadvental age; and (3) the special, powerful presence of the Holy Spirit accompanying and energizing Christians in their kingdom-advancing commission.

On these theses rests the promise of postmillennialism.

CHAPTER 5
CONFESSIONAL POSTMILLENIALISM

ESCHATOLOGY, "the study of the last things or of the future generally,"[1] is a divisive issue, even — perhaps especially — among conservative Christians. The principal source of contention is usually the relation of the second coming of Christ (or, if one is dispensational, also the "rapture" of the church) to the "millennium," the 1000 years of Satan's binding declared in Revelation chapter 20.

As you might have noticed by now, there are numerous shades of eschatological opinions, ranging from dispensational premillennialism, historic premillennialism, amillennialism, "optimistic amillennialism,"[2] and postmillennialism, to particular species of these viewpoints, including pretribulational dispensational premillennialism, midtribulational dispensational premillennialism, posttribulational dispensational premillennialism, and partial rapturism, not to mention preterism. It's a Baskin Robbins 31-flavor eschatology.

The church historic has not devoted nearly as much attention to eschatology as it has to other issues — for example, the Trinity, Christology, and soteriology (the doctrines of personal salvation). The latter issues forming the core of the Christian message were the focal point of theological controversy during the first sixteen centuries of the church; therefore, they have garnered significant creedal attention and formulation. That the church has been less inclined to enshrine in her creeds and confessions a detailed explanation of her eschatological views has led some like Berkhof to conclude,

> Up to the present time . . . the doctrine of the millennium has never yet been embodied in a single Confession, and therefore cannot be regarded as a dogma of the church.[3]

While this comment is true as it stands, the corollary of such sentiment is to convince the historically unwary that one's eschatological views are of no great moment inasmuch as the confessions are agnostic about the issue of eschatology — or at least millennialism.

CONFESSIONS NOT MILLENNIALLY AGNOSTIC

But this conclusion is patently false. For while it is true that neither the creeds of early catholic orthodoxy nor the great confessions of the Reformation era contain a discussion of millennial terms (which, in any case, were not invented until comparatively recently), the eschatological notions of some of the latter documents cannot be understood equally well in any of the three main millennial frameworks (pre- , a- , and post-millennialism).

A chief example is the Larger Catechism of the Westminster Confession of Faith, whose postmillennial eschatology is implicit. For instance, Question 45 asks, "How doth Christ execute the office of a king?" The answer is:

> Christ executeth the office of a king, in calling out of the world a people to himself, and giving them officers, laws, and censures, by which he visibly governs them; in bestowing saving grace on his elect, rewarding them for their obedience,

and correcting them for their sins; preserving and supporting them under all their temptations and sufferings, *restraining and overcoming all their enemies*, and powerfully ordering all things for his own glory, and their good; and also in *taking vengeance on the rest*, who know not God, and obey not the gospel.[4]

There is no room in this answer for an increasingly evil world as posited by dispensationalism[5] and a pessimistic version of amillennialism.[6]

Lest the dispensationalist get the impression that the expressions "restraining and overcoming all their enemies" and "taking vengeance on the rest, who know not God, and obey not the gospel" refer exclusively to Christ's exercise of kingly prerogatives *after* his Second Advent, he should note the answer to Question 42 declaring that Christ "execute[s] the offices of prophet, priest, and, king of his church, in the estate *both* of his humiliation *and* [present] exaltation."[7]

Moreover, lest the amillennialist deduce that these exercises of imperial rule pertain only to the increase of the church and not to the wider society, he should observe the texts the framers of the catechism offer as proof for their assertion: 1 Corinthians 15:25, Psalm 110:1, and, significantly, "the whole Psalm [110] throughout."[8] Verses 5 and 6 of the Psalm state, "The Lord at thy right hand shall strike through kings in the day of his wrath. He shall judge among the heathen, he shall fill the places of the dead bodies; he shall wound the heads over many countries."

Although the language employed here is largely figurative and symbolical, the extent of Christ's rule clearly transcends the church to include the Gentile nations and political rulers.

Further, the answer to query 54, "How is Christ exalted in his sitting at the right hand of God?" includes the statement, "[He] doth gather and defend his church, and subdue her enemies," employing again Psalm 110:1 and "the whole

Psalm throughout" as biblical proof.[9] Obviously implied as enemies that Christ will subdue in his regal authority are the hostile Gentiles and kings of the earth. This subdual, contra dispensationalism, occurs in Christ's *present* session, and contra the pessimistic species of amillennialism, extends beyond the church to include the entire Gentile world.

THE POSTMILL BRITS

The Westminster Larger Catechism, however, is not the only doctrinal standard espousing an eschatology most closely in harmony with postmillennialism. The Savoy Declaration of 1658, "merely a modification of the Westminster Confession to suit the Congregational polity,"[10] was hammered out by English Congregational Calvinists like John Owen. It adds to the Westminster chapter on the church a section V, which reads as follows:

> As the Lord is in care and love towards his church, hath in his infinite wise providence exercised it with great variety in all ages, for the good of them that love him, and his own glory; so, according to his promise, we expect that in the latter days, Antichrist being destroyed,[11] and the adversaries of the kingdom of his dear Son broken, the churches of Christ being enlarged and edified through a free and plentiful communication of light and grace, shall enjoy in this world a more quiet, peaceable, and glorious condition than they have enjoyed.[12]

It is difficult to imagine a more postmillennial statement short of framing the term itself. The original Congregationalists expected "in this world" not merely the destruction of the enemies of the church, but its increase, edification, and peace — just as the prophets of the Old Testament predict.[13]

The Reformed confessions and catechisms are not reticent

or agnostic about the topic of eschatology and, specifically, the millennium, or the course of God's dealings with the church and world. Some of them fully expressed their expectation of the advancement of Christ's kingdom in history before the Second Advent and including the subdual of evil in all the earth.

CONCLUSION

I've noted several times already that in widespread arguments over eschatology, somebody often declares in diffidence (or desperation), "I'm a panmillennialist. All I care about is that everything will 'pan out' on the end."

This response, while understandable, is naïve. One's views on the millennium, and particularly of eschatology in general, shape his entire life.

Eschatology isn't just about last things. It's also about first things. What you believe about eschatology will affect how you live your life.

And the consistent postmillennialist certainly lives his life very differently from the premillennial dispensationalist and the pessimistic version of amillennialist.

CHAPTER 6
CREEDAL ESCHATOLOGY IS BIBLICAL ESCHATOLOGY

BIBLICAL ORTHODOXY (correct belief) is often under attack by alleged believers who claim that since the Bible is the infallible word of God (correct) and the common Christian creeds are not (also correct), the creeds are wrong (incorrect).

Because the Roman and Eastern churches rely on those creeds as dogma, the creed-opposing crowd assumes Protestants don't (or at least shouldn't) view the creeds as authoritative. They fail to grasp that what the Westminster Confession calls "good and necessary consequence" of biblical truth is as binding as biblical truth — because it is.

The orthodox Trinity (for example) is biblical truth summarized as brief systematic theology. That's what all accurate creeds like the Apostles, Nicene, Chalcedonian, and Athanasian are: mini-systematic theologies. This is why the Reformers all affirmed ancient ecumenical creedal Christianity. The fact that creeds do not occupy the precise role in Protestantism they do in Rome and the East doesn't mean we orthodox Protestants deny the authority of those creeds. We do not. Why? Because they summarize biblical truth, which is the final authority.[1]

HERETICAL PRETERISM

Today one vocal heretical sect opposing the creeds in their doctrines of last things (eschatology) is so-called "full" or "consistent," preterism, which should be distinguished from partial preterism:

> Preterism, a Christian eschatological view, interprets some (partial preterism) or all (full preterism) prophecies of the Bible as events which have already happened. This school of thought interprets the Book of Daniel as referring to events that happened from the 7th century BC until the first century AD, while seeing the prophecies of the Book of Revelation as events that happened in the first century AD. Preterism holds that Ancient Israel finds its continuation or fulfillment in the Christian church at the destruction of Jerusalem in AD 70. The term preterism comes from the Latin *praeter*, which is a prefix denoting that something is "past" or "beyond". Adherents of preterism are known as preterists. Preterism teaches that either all (full preterism) or a majority (partial preterism) of the Olivet discourse had come to pass by AD 70.[2]

Full preterism holds that all biblical prophecy was fulfilled in the A. D. 70 destruction of Jerusalem and ancient Judaism. Full preterism must, therefore, deny orthodox Christianity since it denies the *future* (to us) visible, physical return of Christ; the future visible, physical resurrection of the righteous and unrighteous; and the future visible, physical final judgment of both. These doctrines are parts of core, basic Christian belief. For instance, the eschatological portions of the Nicene Creed (shared by all other ecumenical creeds as well as the major Reformation confessions) are these:

> *He [Christ] will come again with glory*
> *to judge the living and the dead.*

His kingdom will never end…
We look forward to the resurrection of the dead,
and to life in the world to come.

Every major Reformation confession — Lutheran, Presbyterian, Congregational, Anglican, Baptist — affirmed these biblical truths. So did Roman Catholicism and Eastern Orthodoxy. In other words, the entire Christian tradition believes these truths. The only quasi-Christian groups that question or deny them are (1) the ancient Gnostics, (2) the more recent anti-supernaturalistic theological liberals, and now, even more recently, (3) the full preterists.

Full preterists deny basic Christian eschatology. Therefore, they're heretics in the most accurate sense of that word. They are *heretical* preterists (hereafter HP).[3] While there is plenty of legitimate disagreement among orthodox Christians on eschatological issues like the millennium, the tribulation mentioned in Daniel, the timing of the future Second Advent, the identification of the Antichrist(s), and the interpretation of Revelation, there is no legitimate disagreement on the basic biblical eschatology of the common Christian creeds.

Many who deny fundamental Christian doctrines like HP's, Arians, and Oneness Pentecostals claim they rely wholly on biblical exegesis, while they assert their orthodox critics rely on the creeds.

This charge is false and disingenuous. The orthodox (especially orthodox Protestants) have done massively more, and more rigorous, exegesis than the heretics. They simply know that the creeds accurately summarize the products of all that faithful exegesis and don't need to re-exegete those passages every time a heretical newbie comes baying for exegesis. Rome and the East assert the creeds are true because they are dogma: *we Protestants assert they are dogma because they are true*.

In this chapter, I'll briefly and simply show three biblical passages (among scores I could mention) that prove the future visible, physical return of Christ. I could do the same for the future visible, physical resurrection and final judgment of the righteous and unrighteous. I'll try to avoid technical language and Greek and Hebrew. I'll write as simply as I can.

I'll also show how arguably the chief HP scholar (actually there are almost no HP scholars, a telling fact) is wrong about these three passages. He is J. Stuart Russell (1816–1895), and the book is *The Parousia*.[4] ("Parousia" means coming or appearing). This book does a masterful job of showing that many passages often assumed to refer to the Second Advent actually refer to God's A. D. 70 judgment-coming.

Unfortunately, Russell claims *all* (or virtually all) of them do. I use this book as a foil because the author is far removed from any present controversy and because the book is considered the bible of HP. (Page numbers from the Russell citations appear in parentheses after them.)

ORTHODOX BIBLICAL ESCHATOLOGY

Acts 1

In Acts 1:10–11, Luke's account of our Lord's ascension, we read:

> *And while they [Jesus' disciples'] looked steadfastly toward heaven as He went up, behold, two men stood by them in white apparel, who also said, "Men of Galilee, why do you stand gazing up into heaven? This* same *Jesus, who was taken up from you into heaven, will so come **in like manner** [or "in just the same way"] as you saw Him go into heaven." (emphasis supplied)*

We can imagine the disciples' joy over their Friend, the risen Lord, tinged with disappointment at his departure —

his very visible and physical departure. God dispatches angels to comfort the disciples with the truth that this very Jesus will return to them one day "in just the same way." Jesus wouldn't simply return to earth; he would return *in the same manner* as he departed — visibly and physically from the heavens.

This obvious interpretation poses problems for the HP's. Jesus did not return visibly and physically in A. D. 70, so if the standard orthodox interpretation of this passage is true, there is a coming or appearing after A. D. 70. Russell asserts:

> There is no indication of time in this parting promise, but it is only reasonable to suppose that the disciples would regard it as addressed to them, and that they would cherish the hope of soon seeing Him again, according to His own saying, 'A little while, and ye shall see me.' This belief sent them back to Jerusalem with great joy. Is it credible that they could have felt this elation if they had conceived that His coming would not take place for eighteen centuries? Or can we suppose that their joy rested upon a delusion? There is no conclusion possible but that which holds the belief of the disciples to have been well founded, and the Parousia nigh at hand. (147–148).

But this assumes what needs to be proved. Russell has already decided that the (final) Parousia happened in A. D. 70, so that's what the angels *must* have been talking about. He shoehorns his theology into the biblical text rather than let the text tell us what, and what kind, of coming it is. If Jesus were to return "in just the same way" as he departed, it can't be the A. D. 70 Parousia but the Second Advent.

Russell argues that this can't be the case, since this now 2000+ year-later Parousia wouldn't have comforted the disciples. This is a strange, self-defeating argument. For *how would a non-physical but fierce judgment Parousia at A. D. 70 comfort them either*? There was no comfort, certainly no visibly present comfort, in A. D. 70. All to the contrary.

But the fact is, according to 1 Thessalonians 4:13–18 (the late R. C. Sproul, a partial preterist, writes that this passage proves a "sharp distinction"[5] between the A. D. 70 and the final Parousia), Christ will return visibly and physically from the heavens and concurrently resurrect the bodies of all deceased saints whose spirits accompany him (including those of the early ascension-witnessing disciples). These deceased saints will, in fact, therefore, see him "in just the same way" as the angels promised. Acts 1 doesn't promise the disciples won't die until they see the Lord again. It does promise they'll see him "in just the same way."

And at the Second Advent, they will.

Hebrews 9

Hebrews 9:27–28 reads:

> *And as it is appointed for men to die once, but after this the judgment, so Christ was offered once to bear the sins of many. To those who eagerly wait for Him He will **appear a second time**, apart from sin, for salvation. (emphasis supplied)*

The author has been extensively arguing the superiority of the new covenant to the old. Here he contrasts the First Advent with the Second. The difference is simple but dramatic: at his first coming (the incarnation), Christ was surrounded and weighed down by sin, not his own, since he was sinless, but ours. This was at the heart of his ministry as the great high priest. The whole point of priesthood is to deal with sin. No priest dealt with it finally and definitively until Jesus Christ. Thus, this First Advent was not "apart from sin." Sin had a claim on all Jesus was and did: "And the Lord [the Father] has laid on Him [Christ] the iniquity of us all" (Isaiah

53:6). This was not Jesus' sin (he was sinless), but our sin that he came to pay for and purge.

But when he returns the second time (this is the closest the Bible comes to referring to the "Second Coming [or Advent]"), he will be entirely "apart from sin." Sin (ours) no longer lays claim to him. He comes to punish the wicked and reward the righteous. This implies the future final judgment. "[T]hose who eagerly wait for Him" are the redeemed. We need not fear the final judgment since our great high priest has been judged on our behalf (substitutionary atonement). But the unrighteous should fear the judgment after their death and after Christ's second coming.

Russell's treatment of these verses is reduced to this single paragraph:

> The attitude of expectation maintained by the Christians of the apostolic age is here incidentally shown. They waited in hope and confidence for the fulfillment of the promise of His coming. To suppose that they thus waited for an event which did not happen is to impute to them and to their teachers an amount of ignorance and error incompatible with respect of their beliefs on any other subject.

In other words, the Second Coming had to have been in A. D. 70 or their hopes would have been dashed. But he doesn't explain why this must be the case. He doesn't seem to envision that a coming they did not see in their lifetime, one after which all the wicked would be judged and all human history set to rights, could also have comforted them. As my colleague Brian Mattson mentioned to me,

> Russell's logic is so bizarre: it is somehow unworthy of the saints to believe in a promise that isn't fulfilled in their lifetimes? That would be …. *Every single Old Testament saint*. It is

a glory of the saints to believe God's promises even if they do not see them fulfilled. Faith 101.

But the greater problem is that a second non-physical coming in Jewish judgment (A. D. 70) is not parallel to a first physical coming in universal redemption. The distinction in this passage between the First and Second Advents was not that the first was physical and the second non-physical, the first was universally significant and the second Judaically significant, but that the first was *not* "apart from sin" and the second will be.

Our Lord is not returning as the earthly sin-bearer but as the heavenly crown-wearer. A. D. 70 was God's judgment on an apostate Israel. Hebrews 9 predicts God's judgment on an entire apostate humanity. As the Athanasian Creed declares:

> *[H]e [Christ] is [presently] seated at the Father's*
> *right hand;*
> *from there he will come to judge the living and the*
> *dead.*
> *At his coming all people will arise bodily*
> *and give an accounting of their own deeds.*
> *Those who have done good will enter eternal life,*
> *and those who have done evil will enter eternal*
> *fire.*

Moreover, of what significance is the phrase "apart from sin" to A. D. 70? This has no relevance to God's judgment on Israel. It does, however, have momentous relevance to the future Second Advent, when Christ returns, not bearing the sins of many, but judging the sins of all the unrepentant.

The Second Coming is the future (to us) visible, physical coming in final redemption of the righteous, and final judgment of the unrighteous.

1 Corinthians 15

In 1 Corinthians 15:22–28, as I pointed out in chapter 4, Paul lays out the basic sequence of new covenant history:

> *But now Christ is risen from the dead,* and *has become the firstfruits of those who have fallen asleep. For since by man* came *death, by Man also* came *the resurrection of the dead. For as in Adam all die, even so in Christ all shall be made alive. But each one in his own order: Christ the firstfruits, afterward those* who are *Christ's **at His coming**. **Then** comes **the end**, when He delivers the kingdom to God the Father, when He puts an end to all rule and all authority and power. For He must reign till He has put all enemies under His feet. The last enemy* that *will be destroyed* is *death. For "He has put all things under His feet." But when He says "all things are put under* Him*," it is evident that He who put all things under Him is excepted. Now **when all things are made subject to Him**, then the Son Himself will also be subject to Him who put all things under Him, that God may be all in all. (emphasis supplied)*

This is part of a larger argument against the idea afflicting the Corinthian church that while Christ was raised, he was such an anomaly that there could be no additional resurrection of the saints (see v. 12): Christ's physical resurrection was the last. But I'm concerned here only with Paul's eschatology.

His basic outline is simple. (1) Christ rose from the dead. He was the first fruits, meaning he was the first of many who would rise (we, the redeemed). (2) Then he reigns from heaven in the present era. (3) Then he comes back to earth. (4) Then he resurrects the saints (this is the final resurrection harvest of which his own resurrection was the first fruits). (5)

A POSTMILLENNIAL PRIMER

Then comes "the end," at which time death itself ("the last enemy") will be vanquished. (6) Then Jesus delivers up his present kingdom to the Father, after he has subjugated all his enemies, including death itself. (7) Then God (in eternity) will be "all in all."

It's obvious the "coming" mentioned is the Second Coming. Why? Because all Christ's enemies haven't yet been subjugated. Because the saints haven't yet been bodily resurrected as Jesus, their first fruits, was. Because death itself hasn't been destroyed. Because Christ is still reigning. To say this coming occurred in A. D. 70 means all these things have already occurred. That view is palpably absurd.

But not for J. Stuart Russell. He must have recognized the problems these verses pose for his view (which he admits is "novel" [199]), because he devotes nine pages to it, while he spends little time on Acts 1 and Hebrews 9. His interpretive contortions consist of these:

1 Christ handed over his kingdom to the Father at A. D. 70. His present reign in heaven is now over. Jesus is no longer earth's reigning King. (204)

2 All enemies subjugated at the Second Coming were the Jewish rulers of the time. The pagan Roman Empire wasn't actually that much of an enemy. All enemies means all *Jewish* enemies in A. D. 70. (204–205) This would have been news to all those Christians in the contemporaneous reign of Nero Caesar (A. D. 54–68) whom he ignited as human torches to illuminate his depraved parties.

3 The destruction of death at the Parousia referred only to the destruction of death to the faithful Jews of the old covenant, not the final judgment of all humanity at the end of history. His reasoning is so bizarre that it warrants a longer citation:

> True, the spiritual and invisible accompaniments of that [A. D. 70] judgment are not recorded by the historian, for they

were not such as the human senses could apprehend or verify; yet what Christian can hesitate to believe that, contemporaneously with the outward judgment of the seen [on Jerusalem], there was a corresponding judgment of the unseen? Such, at least, is the inference fairly deducible from the teachings of the New Testament. That at the great epoch of the [A. D. 70] Parousia the dead as well as the living — not of the whole human race, but of the subjects of the Theocratic [Jewish] kingdom — were to be assembled before the [heavenly] tribunal of judgment, is distinctly affirmed in the Scriptures; the [old covenant Jewish] dead being raised up, and the [old covenant Jewish] living undergoing an instantaneous change. In this recall of the dead to life — the resuscitation of those who throughout the duration of the Theocratic kingdom had become the victims and captives of death — we conceive the 'destruction' of death referred to by St. Paul to consist. (206–207)

So, the dead Jews of the old covenant era were resurrected in (to?) heaven, while the Jews living at the time were "instantaneous[ly] change[d]," despite the fact that no person at the time recorded such a bizarre event of living Jews being resurrected and transported [?] to the invisible heavenly tribunal. This is simply absurd.

According to Russell, we're forced to believe this passage deals exclusively with old covenant Judaism, despite the fact that the entire force of 1 Corinthians 15 is universal and has nothing unique to say to Jews.

We're obliged to accept that Jesus Christ is no longer the ruling King, despite the fact that Philippians 2 tells us that he will rule as Lord until *every* knee, not just every old covenant Jewish knee, bows to him.

We're required to accept that the final resurrection occurred in A. D. 70, that it was a resurrection limited to old covenant Jews, and that the Jews living at the time were resurrected and somehow made to appear before a heavenly tribunal.

This scenario is more bizarre than the most fanciful dispensational interpretation devised.

CONCLUSION

The Bible teaches in these passages (and others) the future, visible, physical Second Coming of our presently reigning Lord. The common Christian creeds assert this basic biblical truth and others. Every orthodox Christian in history has eagerly affirmed them. Many of us confess them every Sunday. No orthodox Christian would deny them.

And we biblical Protestants affirm them precisely because the Bible teaches them.

The Bible alone is the final authority, but not the Bible and you or I alone in our basement cut off from the church historic and everybody else who ever interpreted it. We Protestants affirm the priesthood of all believers, not the priesthood of each believer isolated from every other one.

War on the Christian Worldview

Recall the Christian worldview summarized as creation–fall-redemption. The eschaton (conclusion of history) and its events like the future visible, physical return of Christ; the future visible, physical resurrection of the righteous and unrighteous; and the future visible, physical final judgment of both constitute the culmination of our Lord's great work of redemption. Without them, there is no redemption. Creation and eschaton are the bookends of the Christian worldview. To deny the eschaton is no less fatal to the Christian worldview than to deny creation. HP, therefore, is at war with the Christian worldview.

Therefore, *stand fast* in the Faith once for all definitively delivered to the saints (Jude 3). There is yet more truth to be mined from the Bible.

But no biblical truth undermines the core Faith all Christians confess. Few writers have expressed this point as potently and eloquently as the great 19th century church historian Phillip Schaff in *The Principle of Protestantism*, and I'll conclude with it:

> [T]he case of the *formal* dogmatic tradition … is such as **has not for its contents something different from what is contained in the Bible**, but forms the channel by which these contents are conducted forward in history; the onward development thus of church doctrine and church life, as comprehended first dogmatically in the so-called rules of faith, above all in the Apostles' Creed, and then the ecumenical creeds — the Nicene and Athanasian — and still further as orally carried forward, apart from all written statement, through the entire course of church history, so that everyone, before he wakes to self-consciousness, is made involuntarily to feel its power. Tradition **in this sense** is absolutely indispensable [and unavoidable, PAS]. By this means **we come first to the contents of the Bible**; and from it these draw their life for us, perpetually fresh and new; in such a way that Christ and his apostles are made present, and speak to us directly, in the Spirit which breathes in the Bible, and flows through the church in her life's blood. *This tradition therefore is not a part of a divine word separately from that which is written, but* **the contents of scripture itself** *as apprehended and settled by the church* **against heresies past and always new appearing**; *not an independent source of revelation, but* **the one fountain of the written word**, *only rolling itself forward in the stream of church consciousness*. (bold emphases supplied, italics original)[6]

EPILOGUE: WHY WE WILL WIN

"Do you believe in God, Winston?"

"No."

"And do you consider yourself a man?"

"Yes."

"If you are a man, Winston, you are the last man.

Your kind is extinct; we are the inheritors."

George Orwell, Nineteen Eighty-Four

THE MOTHER OF ALL CONSPIRACIES

A decrepit age is governed by conspiracy thought. It blames the politicians, blacks, Jews, capitalists, communists, Christians, socialists, and almost any other race, religion, class or group for imaginary or actual evils. Its practitioners are not interested in righteous dominion. They are interested in "escapegoating": vesting blame for and "objectifying" all the evil in the world in or as a certain group, race, or religion. Escapegoating conveniently diverts attention from one's own sins and failures so he can elude personal responsibility; it is the ultimate motivation of conspiracy thought.

Ultimately there is only one global conspiracy. The mother of all conspiracies — at least the only conspiracy of any consequence — is related in the Bible in Genesis 3. In this text is recorded Satan's employment of the serpent to subvert God's eternal plan for man: a righteous race exerting dominion in the earth under God's authority (Gen. 1:26-28).

Satan offered to Eve an easier route: procurement of godlike knowledge, dominion without obedience, *power without ethics*. He seduced Eve to decide for herself what is good and what is evil, to refuse submission to divinely revealed authority and arrogate to herself the role of final arbiter of truth. As Van Til notes: "At the instigation of Satan man decided to set himself up as the ultimate standard of right and wrong, of the true and false. He made himself, instead of God, the final reference point in predication."[1]

THE RIGHTEOUS INHERIT

By this tack Satan conspired with Adam and Eve to undercut the godly dominion commission. *All men bear within them the dominion impulse.* Man is made in the image of God; God governs all things (Ps. 47). Man is shaped as governor of the earth, subject to divine authority, God's representative or vicegerent (2 Cor. 5:20). This is why God expelled Adam and Eve from Eden; had they eaten of the Tree of Life they would have obtained eternal life as covenant-beakers (Gen. 3:22-24), maintaining the innate dominion impulse with the ability to exert dominion in terms of their disobedient state. *It is not God's intent that the ungodly exert long-term dominion in the earth* (Ps. 37:9). Adam and Eve must not enjoy eternal life as covenant-beakers. It is God's object that only the righteous inherit the earth (Ps. 37:11). Satan's tactic was to employ the unrighteous to inherit the earth under his sinful influence and control (Eph. 2:1-3; Rom. 6:16; 2 Tim. 2:25, 26).

It remains the conspiracy of Satan to subvert God's plan in the earth. It is fueled by sinful man's notion that man can inherit the earth without God and his word. Man labors to obtain (or create) paradise without God. If he is on the Left in the West during the twenty-first century, he strives for a centralized civic order of equalized wealth and status enforced by political decree.[2] If he is on the Right he works for a traditional heirarchical order and a bland generic morality to keep anarchic ("market-threatening") impulses in check.[3] In either case, covenant-breaking man wants a world in which the Triune God expressing himself infallibly in Holy Scripture is sealed away hermetically in the far reaches of the universe, leaving apostate, dominion-minded man free rein to shape his own destiny.

The problem is basic: ungodly men exerting ungodly dominion in terms of their ungodly faith. Satan's purpose is clear: he wants the ungodly to inherit the earth, subject to his authority (Lk. 4:5, 6).

For Satan, the ungodly, not the godly, must inherit.

THE DIVERSION OF THE CHURCH

The church, by its omission of responsible dominion work, has abetted ungodly men and Satan in their ungodly dominion. For two millennia the church has been often plagued by man-centered thought supposedly "Christ- (or Cross- or Gospel-) centered," but in actuality truncated, pietist, and humanist.

It is most often manifested in the idea that biblical faith is principally about man's personal salvation; it frequently is wedded to a mystical tradition, an attempt to escape the troubles of life, the wear and tear of history, and secure an eternally timeless, subjectively pious, exclusively vertical religion on earth. It fails to see that the gospel and soteriology are not the end of God's plan for man; but the *means* to an end. The actual end is the subordination of all things to God through Christ by means of the earthly dominion of the godly. God's purpose is not chiefly to save man and fit him for heaven, but to restore him to covenant-keeping submission and his calling as God's dominion agent in the earth. Heaven on earth in eternity is the blissful culmination of this task faithfully prosecuted by the redeemed.

The patristic church developed, and the medieval church completed, the institutionalization of the Christian Faith in the church.[4] In the fourth century under Constantine, the great imperial authority, the Faith conquered the Roman Empire; but the Faith was increasingly aligned with the institutional hierarchy of the Roman Catholic Church. In the East the Faith was progressively mystical and subservient to the emperor and state.[5]

In the West, however, the Protestant Reformation reversed this diversion, restoring the Faith to its wide application. The Reformation re-exalted the godly man as the godly man, and not as the appendage to the institutional church. The righteous man's vocation apart from the church was considered no less holy than the priesthood or clergy. The Reformation, especially the Reformed tradition, took seriously man's calling in the earth.

THE INHERITANCE OF THE GODLY

Why is man on earth? He exists to glorify God (1 Cor. 10:31). But why *specifically* was man placed here? What is the chief *means* by which he is to glorify God? The Bible is clear on this question. God placed man on earth to exert dominion under God's authority (Gen. 1:26-28; 9:1 f.; Ps. 8).

Because man sinned and polluted his commission, God in his grace deigned in love to send his only begotten Son, Jesus Christ, as the New Adam to succeed where the first Adam failed (Rom. 5:12f.). Christ became the ultimate Dominion Man: this is why the Epistle to Hebrews ascribes to Christ the dominion calling originally given to man (Heb. 2:5-8). Jesus Christ is the seed of the woman whose feet will crush the head of the seed of the serpent (Gen. 3:15; see chapter 4). He is victor. All united to him by faith, whose sins have been atoned for in his sacrificial death and justified by his resurrection (1 Cor. 15:1-4; Rom. 4:25) join in his present dominion reign (Rom. 8:17; Eph. 1:18-23).

THE FINAL CONQUEST

The Bible does not promise that God will expel all evil before the Second Advent. Only at Christ's Second Advent will the last enemy, death, be banished (1 Cor. 15:26). As this primer has shown, however, the Bible does promise that God by his word will progressively curtail evil in the world, though postmillennialism is not a utopian vision. Bloesch observes:

> If we abandon the world to the devil, the devil who has been dethroned will seize the opportunity to regain his power, and this has happened ever again when Christians have been lulled to sleep by a false pietism, which is, in effect, quietism. We need to recover the robust and expectant faith of the original evangelicals, whose missionary enthusiasm was accompanied by an outpouring of humanitarian and social reform. We need to recover the postmillennial vision of the church on the march, without succumbing to any kind of utopianism and false romanticism.[45]

"Utopianism and false romanticism" would include the

EPILOGUE: WHY WE WILL WIN

hopeful but naive assumption that the kingdom will advance painlessly without Christians' hardy effort.

The Bible is clear, however, that "through much tribulation [we] enter into the kingdom of God" (Ac. 14:22). The measure of kingdom advancement is the measure of Christian effort. There is no room for a Christian army that craves victories without battles, glory without pain.

Nonetheless, God employs his righteous seed as his representatives, his vicegerents, to claim the world for Christ the King, to steward the earth, to possess the kingdom in all realms, with his inscripturated word as their guide and inspiration.

We Christians are *entitled* to the possession of the earth as Christ's joint-heirs (Rom. 8:17), ruling and reigning with him (Rev. 1:5, 6) as a result of his sovereign, predestinating grace (Eph. 1).

Satan and his seed and hosts will not overthrow the kingdom of God's dear Son. The stone cut out without hands will swell to fill the earth. The mustard seed will grow to a wondrous tree, housing the birds of the earth. The yeast will leaven the entire dough. Christ will reign until all his enemies are placed under his feet in submission. The saints of the most high *will* possess the kingdom. The wicked *cannot* inherit.

We are the inheritors.

NOTES

INTRODUCTION

1. Millard Erickson, *Contemporary Options in Eschatology* (Grand Rapids: Baker, 1977).

1. THE DEFECT OF DISPENSATIONALISM

1. Clarence B. Bass, *Backgrounds to Dispensationalism* (Grand Rapids: Eerdmans, 1960), 64–140.
2. Mark Sweetnam and Crawford Gribben, "J. N. Darby and the Irish Origins of Dispensationalism," *Journal of the Evangelical Theological Society*, 52/3 [September, 2009], 576.
3. Thomas D. Ice, "What Is Progressive Dispensationalism?" https://digitalcommons.liberty.edu/cgi/viewcontent.cgi?article=1118&context=pretrib_arch, accessed March 24, 2023.
4. See O. Palmer Robertson, *The Christ of the Covenants* (Phillipsburg, New Jersey: Presbyterian and Reformed, 1980).
5. Robert P. Lightner, "A Dispensational Response to Theonomy," *Bibliotheca Sacra*, 143/571 [July-September, 1986], 235.
6. Dwight Pentecost, *Things to Come* (Grand Rapids: Zondervan [1958], 1964), 9-15.
7. Walter C. Kaiser, Jr. *Toward Rediscovering the Old Testament* (Grand Rapids: Zondervan, 1987), ch. 7.
8. Jaroslav Pelikan, *The Emergence of the Catholic Tradition* (Chicago and London: University of Chicago Press, 1971), 81.
9. Oswald Allis, *Prophecy and the Church* (Phillipsburg, NJ: Presbyterian and Reformed [1945, 1947], 1978), 49.
10. John Gerstner, *Wrongly Dividing the Word of Truth: A Critique of Dispensationalism* (Brentwood, TN: Wolgemuth & Hyatt, 1991), 186, See also the nondispensational premillennialist George E. Ladd, *Crucial Questions About the Kingdom of God* (Grand Rapids: Zondervan, 1952), 153–158.
11. Charles Ryrie, *Dispensationalism Today* (Chicago: Moody, 1965), 47.
12. *Ibid.*, 44, 45.
13. *Ibid.*, 137-140.
14. Daniel P. Fuller, *Gospel and Law: Contrast or Continuum—The Hermeneutics of Dispensationalism and Covenant Theology* (Grand Rapids: Eerdmans, 1980), 189-197, and Vern S. Poythress, *Understanding Dispensationalists* (Grand Rapids: Zondervan, 1987) 44, 45.
15. John Murray, *Epistle to the Romans* (Grand Rapids: Eerdmans, 1965), 2:95.

NOTES

16. Walter C. Kaiser, Jr., "Response to Greg L. Bahnsen," in *The Law, the Gospel, and the Modern Christian*, Wayne G. Strickland, ed. (Grand Rapids, 1993), 152.
17. Fuller, *Gospel and Law*, ch. 5.
18. Dispensationalist John Walvoord says, "It is recognized by all serious students of the Bible that the covenant of God with Abraham is one of the important and determinative relations of Scripture. It furnishes the key to the entire Old Testament and reaches for its fulfillment into the New," *The Millennial Kingdom* (Findlay, OH: Dunham, 1959), 139.
19. The passage of Gal. 3 (as well as Ac. 15 and Col. 2:14–23) indicates what aspect of the Mosaic law has been canceled; those rites and ceremonies which erected a barrier between ethnic Israel and the Gentiles. The NT nowhere cancels or supersedes the moral aspects of the law, and even the "general equity" (Westminster Confession of Faith language) of the judicial aspects of the OT law remains in force. See Daniel P. Fuller, *The Unity of the Bible* (Grand Rapids: Zondervan, 1992), 362.
20. Fuller, *Gospel and Law*, 165-168; see also George Eldon Ladd, *The Last Things: An Eschatology for Laymen* (Grand Rapids: Eerdmans, 1978) chap. 2.
21. Walter C. Kaiser, Jr., "The Place of Law and Good Works in Evangelical Christianity," in *A Time to Speak*, A. James Rudin and Marvin R. Wilson, eds. (Grand Rapids: Eerdmans, 1987), 124.
22. Gerstner, *Wrongly Dividing the Word of Truth*, 195, 196. Also O. Palmer Robertson, "Hermeneutics of Continuity," in *Continuity and Discontinuity*, John S. Feinberg, ed. (Westchester, Illinois: crossway, 1988), chap. 4.
23. Heinrich Bullinger, *A Brief Exposition of the One Eternal Testament or Covenant of God*, in *Fountainhead of Federalism*, Charles S. McCoy and Wayne Baker, eds. (Louisville, Kentucky: Westminster/John Knox Press, 1991), 111.
24. This does not mean that there are not glorious covenant promises to the physical, covenant seed of True Israel, the church of whatever race. See Andrew Murray, *How To Raise Your Children for Christ* (Minneapolis: Bethany House, 1975).

2. THE PROBLEM OF PREMILLENNIALISM

1. See George Eldon Ladd, *A Commentary on the Revelation* (Grand Rapids: Eerdmans, 1972), ch. 20.
2. George Eldon Ladd, "Historic Premillennialism," in *The Meaning of the Millennium: Four Views*, Robert G. Clouse, ed. (Downers Grove, IL, 1977), 17–40.
3. Marcellus J. Kik. *An Eschatology of Victory* (no loc.: Presbyterian and Reformed, 1975), 179–196.
4. David Chilton, "Will the Real Literalist Please Stand Up?", *Chalcedon Report*, July, 1996, 10-12.

NOTES

3. THE ANOMALY OF AMILLENNIALISM

1. Philip Edgcumbe Hughes, *The Book of Revelation* (Grand Rapids: Eerdmans, 1990), 208–216.
2. Bruce K. Waltke, *Genesis* (Grand Rapids: Zondervan, 2001), 93–94.
3. This is a foretaste of the final, definitive new heavens and earth mentioned in Revelation 21: 1–4.
4. Louis Berkhof, *Systematic Theology* (Grand Rapids: Eerdmans [1939], 1941), 718,719.
5. For a postmillennial explanation, see Loraine Boettner, *The Millennium* (no loc.: Presbyterian and Reformed, 1957), 353–356.
6. Greg L. Bahnsen, *Victory in Jesus* (Texarkana, Arkansas, Covenant Media, 1999), 12.

4. THE PROMISE OF POSTMILLENNIALISM

1. John Murray, *The Epistle to the Romans* (Grand Rapids: Eerdmans, 1965), 1:143, bold emphasis supplied.
2. Even the arch-dispensationalist C.I. Scofield admitted this: *The Scofield Reference Bible* (New York: Oxford University Press, 1909), 900, 901.
3. Greg L. Bahnsen and Kenneth L. Gentry, Jr., *House Divided: The Break-Up of Dispensational Theology* (Tyler, TX: Institute for Christian Economics, 1989) 213-217, and William Symington, *Messiah the Prince, or The Mediatorial Dominion of Jesus Christ* (Edmonton, Canada: Still Waters Revival Books [1884], 1990.
4. Loraine Boettner, *The Millennium* (no loc.: Presbyterian and Reformed, 1957), 38-47.
5. John Calvin, *Commentaries on the Epistle of Paul the Apostle to the Hebrews* (Grand Rapids: Baker, 1993), 60.
6. James Bannerman, *The Church of Christ* (Edmonton, Alberta, Canada: Still Waters Revival Books [1869], 1991), 2:8-12.
7. See Kenneth Gentry, *The Greatness of the Great Commission* (Tyler, TX: Institute of Christian Economics, 1990).

5. CONFESSIONAL POSTMILLENIALISM

1. Millard Erickson, *Concise Dictionary of Christian Theology* (Grand Rapids: Baker, 1986), 50. This chapter concerns cosmic, rather than individual, eschatology, the former referring to God's plan for the human race and earth collectively, and the latter referring to God's plan for converted and unconverted individuals.
2. This optimistic version reflects the same method of interpretation as well as practical implications of postmillennialism, so it is barely a separate category.

NOTES

3. Louis Berkhof, *The History of Christian Doctrines* (Edinburgh: Banner of Truth [1937], 1969), 264.
4. *Westminster Confession of Faith* (Glasgow: Free Presbyterian Publications [1646], 1958), 149-150, emphases supplied.
5. Dwight Pentecost, *Things To Come* (Grand Rapids: Zondervan, 1958), 155.
6. Herman A. Hoyt, "Amillennialism," in *The Meaning of the Millennium: Four Views*, Robert G. Clouse, ed. (Downers Grove, IL: InterVarsity Press), 1977, 187.
7. *Westminster Confession of Faith*, 148, emphasis supplied.
8. Ibid., 150.
9. Ibid., 155.
10. Philip Schaff, *The Creeds of Christendom* (Grand Rapids: Baker [1931], 1990), 718.
11. The Reformation confessions all identify the Antichrist as the pope or the Roman church. I disagree with this interpretation, but I do not disagree with their optimistic eschatology.
12. Ibid., 723. A similar explication is found in the answer to Question 191 of the Westminster Larger Catechism.
13. For additional defenses of postmillennialism, see John Jefferson Davis, *Christ's Victorious Kingdom* (Grand Rapids: Baker, 1986); J. Marcellus Kik, *An Eschatology of Victory* (no location: Presbyterian and Reformed, 1975); and Kenneth Gentry, *He Shall Have Dominion* (Tyler, TX: Institute for Christian Economics, 1992).

6. CREEDAL ESCHATOLOGY IS BIBLICAL ESCHATOLOGY

1. For more on this, read Jaroslav Pelikan, *Obedient Rebels* (New York and Evanston: Harper & Row, 1964).
2. "Preterism," Scholarly Community Encyclopedia, https://encyclopedia.pub/entry/28866, accessed March 23, 2023.
3. For a thorough refutation see Kenneth L. Gentry, Jr., *Have We Missed the Second Coming? A Critique of the Hyper-Preterist Error* (Fountain Inn, SC: Victorious Hope Publishing, 2016).
4. J. Stuart Russell, *The Parousia* (Grand Rapids: Baker, 1983, 1999).
5. R. C. Sproul, *The Last Days According to Jesus* (Grand Rapids: Baker, 1988).
6. Phillip Schaff, *The Principle of Protestantism* (Philadelphia and Boston: United Church Press, 1964), 115–116.

EPILOGUE: WHY WE WILL WIN

1. Cornelius Van Til, *A Christian Theory of Knowledge* (Phillipsburg, NJ: Presbyterian and Reformed, 1969), 47.
2. J.G. Meriquor, *Liberalism Old and New* (Boston: Twayne, 1991), 99f.
3. Roger Scruton, *Conservatism* (New York: All Points Books, 2017).

NOTES

4. Philip Schaff, *Medieaval Christianity: A.D. 590-1073* (Grand Rapids: Eerdmans, 1910), 13.
5. Michael W. Kelley, *The Impulse of Power* (Minneapolis: Contra Mundum Books, 1998).

BIBLIOGRAPHY

Allis, Oswald. *Prophecy and the Church*. Phillipsburg, NJ: Presbyterian and Reformed, 1978.

Bahnsen, Greg L. "Confidence About the Earthly Triumph of Christ's Kingdom." *Journey*, March-April 1988.

———. *Victory in Jesus: The Bright Hope of Postmillennialism*. Texarkana, AR: Covenant Media, 1999.

Bass, Clarence B. *Backgrounds to Dispensationalism*. Grand Rapids: Eerdmans, 1960.

Boettner, Loraine. *The Millennium*. no location: Presbyterian and Reformed, 1957.

Boot, Joseph. *The Mission of God: A Manifesto of Hope for Society*. Toronto: Ezra Press, 2016.

———. *Ruler of Kings: Toward a Christian Vision of Government*. London: Wilberforce Publications, 2022.

Brown, David. *Christ's Second Coming: Will It Be Premillennial?* Edmonton, Alberta: Still Waters Revival Books [1882], 1990.

Campbell, Roderick. *Israel and the New Covenant*. Philadelphia: Presbyterian and Reformed, 1954.

Clark, David Scott. *The Message from Patmos*. Philadelphia: Bethel Presbyterian Church, n.d.

Clouse, Robert G., ed. *The Meaning of the Millennium: Four Views*. Downers Grove, IL: InterVarsity, 1977

Dabney, Robert L. *Lectures in Systematic Theology*. Grand Rapids: Zondervan [1878], 1972, 837-841.

Davis, John Jefferson. *Christ's Victorious Kingdom*. Grand Rapids, Baker, 1986.

Edwards, Jonathan. *The Works of Jonathan Edwards*. Edinburgh: Banner of Truth Trust [1834], 1974.

Erickson, Millard. *Contemporary Options in Eschatology*. Grand Rapids: Baker, 1977.

Feinberg, John S., ed. *Continuity and Discontinuity*. Westchester, Illinois: Crossway, 1988.

Gentry, Jr., Kenneth L. *Have We Missed the Second Coming? A Critique of the Hyper-Preterist Error*. Fountain Inn, SC: Victorious Hope Publishing, 2016.

———. *He Shall Have Dominion*. Tyler, TX: Institute for Christian Economics, 1992.

Gerstner, John. *Wrongly Dividing the Word of Truth: A Critique of Dispensationalism*. Brentwood, TN: Wolgemuth & Hyatt, 1991.

Hodge, Charles. *Systematic Theology*. Grand Rapids. Eerdmans, 1981, 3:800-807.

BIBLIOGRAPHY

Kaiser, Jr., Walter C. *Toward Rediscovering the Old Testament*. Grand Rapids: Zondervan, 1987.

Kik, J. Marcellus. *An Eschatology of Victory*. no location: Presbyterian and Reformed, 1975.

Marsden, George M. *Fundamentalism and American Culture*. Oxford: Oxford University Press, 1980.

Mathison, Keith A. *Postmillennialism: An Eschatology of Hope*. Phillipsburg, NJ: P&R Publishing, 1999.

Murray, Iain. *The Puritan Hope*. Edinburgh: Banner of Truth Trust, 1971.

Pentecost, Dwight. *Things to Come*. Grand Rapids: Zondervan, [1958], 1964, 9–15.

Poythress, Vern. *Understanding Dispensationalists*. Grand Rapids: Zondervan, 1987.

Provan, Charles. *The Church is Israel Now: The Transfer of Covenant Privilege*. Vallecito, CA: Ross House Books, 1987.

Robertson, O. Palmer. *Christ of the Covenants*. Phillipsburg, New Jersey: Presbyterian and Reformed, 1980.

Rushdoony, R. J., *God's Plan for Victory*. Fairfax, VA: Thoburn Press, 1980.

Ryrie, Charles. *Dispensationalism Today*. Chicago: Moody, 1965.

Symington, William. *Messiah the Prince*. Edmonton, Alberta: Still Waters Revival Books [1884], 1990.

Wright, N. T. *Surprised By Hope: Rethinking Heaven, the Resurrection, and the Mission of the Church*. New York: HarperOne, 2008.

ABOUT THE CENTER FOR CULTURAL LEADERSHIP

The Center for Cultural Leadership (CCL) believes that culture should be Christian — not by political coercion, but by spiritual conversion. Salvation in Jesus Christ should transform all of life.

Christian is what Western culture was for 1000 years, and this is what it should be today. But we're not looking to restore the Christian past, although we are grateful for all its benefits to us. Instead, we want Christian truth to reshape our present and future culture.

But if there's to be Christian culture, Christians must lead it — as fathers, mothers, artists, musicians, college students, businessmen and -women, attorneys, pastors, educators, software writers, salesmen, technicians, politicians, physicians, clerks, and every other life calling.

CCL doesn't so much train Christian activists (lots of people are doing that, and some are doing it effectively). Instead, we're educating and equipping Christian transformationists. It's not enough to be active; you actually have to transform things by a renewed Christian imagination. This is what we're after — Christians whose thinking and lives are transformed so that they, by the Spirit's power, can transform our culture.

In this way, CCL is spearheading a new Christian culture.

Center for Cultural Leadership
P. O. Box 100
Coulterville, CA 95311
831-420-7230
www.christianculture.com

ABOUT THE AUTHOR

P. Andrew Sandlin (B.A., M.A., S.T.D.) is Founder & President of the Center for Cultural Leadership. He is a cultural theologian and an ordained gospel minister in the Nicene Covenant Church and Fellowship of Mere Christianity. He and his wife Sharon have five adult children and five grandchildren.

Printed in Great Britain
by Amazon